Summary Of

The Plant Paradox

The

Hidden Dangers In

Healthy Foods That Cause Disease

And Weight Gain By Dr. Steven R Gundry

Alexander Jones

Copyright ©2018

Disclaimer

This publication is designed to provide competent and reliable information regarding the subject matter covered in The Plant Paradox. This guide is unofficial and is by no means authorized, approved, licensed or endorsed by the original book's author or publisher. **It merely serves as a** *summary and a complementary companion* **to the great work done by Dr. Steven Gundry in the book** *The Plant Paradox.* The author specifically disclaims any liability that is incurred from the use or application of the contents of this book.

You Can Purchase The Plant Paradox From Here

Table of Contents

Executive Summary

The Plant Paradox by Dr. Steven R. Gundry exposes the hidden dangers in plants and animal meat that are making people fat and sick. The book goes beyond textbook explanations of key substances and ingredients in foods recommended in the standard American diet. It introduces the highly toxic plant-based protein called lectin and how it destroys the equilibrium in the gut flora (i.e. the bacteria and other organisms that live inside the intestines), thereby paving the way for *bad* bacteria to infiltrate the body.

The aim of the book is to educate people about foods that are commonly regarded as healthy but are actually designed by nature and evolution to harm people that consume them. What is alarming is that foods that fall under this category are included in several dietary regimens whose goal is to achieve optimum health and wellness.

This is a book written for people to understand why they are not losing weight despite their best efforts. It is also for patients who are diagnosed with diabetes, cancer, and autoimmune diseases so that they can better understand the diseases that plague them and find the right solution to reverse their effects. **It is not written to favor one diet regimen over the other, but to illuminate the dangers that lurk in seemingly healthy foods.** It is not a miracle cure that immediately takes effect, but a gradual progression that involves learning about one's body and how it reacts to certain foods. It is a journey and not a race to the finish line.

Through the Plant Paradox Program, Dr. Gundry hopes to debunk myths, explain the true nature of plants, and expose the agricultural and industrial practices that are causing more harm than good. It offers a solution by providing substitute ingredients, teaching detox processes, developing lectin-free recipes, and showing how to enjoy plant-based meals.

Part 1

The Dietary Dilemma

Chapter 1

The War Between Plants and Animals

For hundreds of millions of years, plant foods are consumed to nourish the body. They are regarded as healthy foods that can sustain the body's nutritional requirements. They provide an abundance of nutrients that allow the body to live and thrive. Anyone who refutes the healing and nurturing properties of plants would most likely find themselves in the minority. After all, edible plants are packed with vitamins and minerals. It would be unthinkable to consider plants as enemies. Perhaps this is because it's hard to imagine that plants have their own defense mechanisms against humans and animals that are out to eat them. Plants don't just grow and await their fate; they also resist.

The Plant Paradox Program has been in existence for over 15 years. The bedrock of the program is the consumption of the right plant foods. To better appreciate the program, there is a need for a re-education about fruits and vegetables. A surprising revelation from the program is that the reduction in the consumption of certain fruits and vegetables from an individual's diet contributed to a better health profile. Kidney function and cholesterol markers have improved dramatically. This goes against a commonly held belief that plant foods are good for the body. Therein lies the paradox.

The contradiction can be easier to fathom if one is willing to unlearn and forget common beliefs about plant foods. It requires a shift in thinking and it starts in changing the way plants are perceived. Plants have always been considered as a harmless source of nourishment. There's this notion that they are generally safe to consume. They give sustenance, so they couldn't be considered enemies. However, plants, like every living thing, possess survival instincts. This means that plants treat plant eaters as enemies and they have a built-in defense system to prevent plant eaters from devouring them and their offspring.

The defense system comes in the form of substances released by plants that are harmful to plant eaters i.e. animals and humans. One shining example of this is **gluten**. It is a plant component that wreaks havoc to the body causing health problems to people who do not have the capacity to process it properly. It is the reason for the emergence of gluten-free movement all over the world. Another example is **lectin**, which is problematic for some people.

The reality is that plants don't want to get eaten and they discourage plant eaters from doing so. Their goal is to propagate their species, much like the humans. So, they protect themselves and their offspring from predators. In the animal world, the predator versus prey system is easy to understand—when the predator attacks, the prey runs. Outrunning the predator is a survival instinct that animals share with humans.

When the prey is an immobile plant, running is not an option. That is not to say plants are helpless and powerless to ward off their prey. They have evolved and developed an assortment of defensive strategies to protect themselves and safeguard their little seeds.

Some plants have the ability to camouflage and blend into their surroundings through their color. They have an array of physical deterrents to keep insects, animals, and humans at bay. Some plants release sticky substances like saps and resins to entangle insects, while others use their natural hard outer coating as protection, like coconut and artichoke. There are also plants that use their texture so that they are unpleasant to eat. These are just a few examples of aggressive tactics to deter plant eaters.

On the subtler side of defensive strategies, plants use biological warfare against predators. They poison, paralyze, or disorient using the natural chemicals in their composition. Plants predate plant eaters. In fact, insects who feast on plants and seeds arrived 90 years after plants appeared 450 million years ago. Insects became the first predators that threatened the existence of plants. Plants evolved to develop lectins that they used to paralyze the insects that fed on them. The same thing holds true in the present day. Although there is a huge difference in size between insects and mammals, both are susceptible to the same effects. Humans may not immediately be paralyzed within minutes of consuming lectin, but they are certainly not immune to the long-term effects.

Lectins have the potential to kill people who have an extreme reaction upon ingestion. An example would be a peanut allergy. Peanuts are high in lectins, so consuming it can be fatal to those who are extremely allergic.

It may not be obvious, but plants are master manipulators. Seeds are actually the babies of the plants. It is safe to say that they are plants in the making. Their potential to become full-grown plants is threatened each day. There are more seeds being produced than will ever take root due to numerous reasons.

There are actually two types of seeds: one that plants want predators to eat and the other is the naked seeds. Those seeds that plants willingly give to the predators are encased in hard shell or coating so that they can pass through the gastrointestinal (GI) tract unscathed. They will remain intact because they are protected. When they emerge from the animal mixed with excrement, they have a chance to sprout and become plants themselves. This is why plants willingly feed them to animals. In fact, they want the protected seeds to be attractive to animals to encourage them to eat it. In addition, animals, being mobile, also help the plant cover more geographical area. Be that as it may, plants will only allow their seeds to be eaten when their protective coverings are completely hardened. Otherwise, the plants will send signals by increasing toxin levels to make it more obvious that the seed is not yet ready for consumption.

Plants use color to communicate to plant eaters that their fruit is ready for harvest or not. They will only give the go signal when they are sure that the mature seed hull has completely hardened, so it can go through the digestive tract unharmed. Green means it's not yet ready and red (or yellow) means it's good to go. If a fruit is harvested while it's still unripe, the lectin content is high. But when it is allowed to ripen naturally, the plant reduces the lectin content in the fruit and skin. Fruits that are picked before they are ready and given the ethylene oxide treatment to make them look ripe still have high lectin content. Humans can fool other humans, but plants know better.

On the other hand, the naked seeds or "naked babies" do not have the same protection so they are more vulnerable. Plants don't want their *naked babies* to be eaten. Plants that grow in the open fields are already in their fertile spot, so they want their naked seeds to take root there when the time comes for the plants to die off. This happens in the winter when plants succumb to the cold weather and thick snow. The seeds are expected to sprout to replace the plants the following season. Without hard coats and casings, the naked seeds are vulnerable to insects, animals, and humans. But it does not mean they do not have a defense system in place. To discourage predators, the naked seeds have to use one or more chemicals to weaken their predators by making them sick. The idea is to teach them a lesson so that they won't attempt to make the same mistake again. The chemicals in seeds include phytates or "antinutrients", trypsin inhibitors, and lectins.

Phytates prevent the absorption of minerals in the diet, which can cause nutritional deficiency. Trypsin inhibitors interfere with the digestive enzymes and prevent it from working properly. Lectins disrupt the cellular communications thus causing gaps in the intestinal wall barrier. These defensive substances are present in whole grains. They can be found in the husk, bran, and fibrous hull.

Other weapons in the bio warfare arsenal are tannins and alkaloids. Tannins are responsible for giving plants a bitter taste. Alkaloids, on the other hand, are highly inflammatory. They are found in stems and leaves of the nightshade family including tomatoes, potatoes, peppers etc. They are also found in beans, legumes, and goji berries.

All these defensive tactics reveal what plants are capable of plotting against those that threaten their existence. It might seem a little farfetched, but from an evolutionary and survival standpoint, it makes a whole lot of sense. Besides, research studies show that plants know when they are being eaten and they consequently increase the production of their toxins to stop and deter their predators. What's even more fascinating is that plants respond to *circadian rhythms*. Plants unleash insecticides at a particular time of day that coincides with the time the predator is likely to attack.

Among all the substances emitted by plants when they are threatened, lectins are particularly harmful to humans. Lectins are large proteins found in both plants and animals. Plants use them as a lethal weapon to defend themselves against predators, especially humans.

Lectins were discovered in 1884 but have not yet achieved the celebrity status of its equally notorious sibling, gluten. Lectins bind to complex sugars and sialic acid, which can be found in the brain, the gut, nerve endings, joints, and blood vessel linings. **This binding process disrupts messaging between cells and causes toxic and inflammatory reactions.** Those who are more sensitive to lectins are much more vulnerable to viruses and bacterial infections.

Aside from the potential health risks, lectins can also cause weight gain. In fact, wheat carries weight-gaining propensity because of the lectin called wheat germ agglutinin (WGA). It was consumed in the ancient times when food is scarce. The same effect of lectin holds true to this day. However, ancient humans were better at dealing with the problem brought on by lectins. Modern humans, instead of completely avoiding the effects of lectin, would invent something to fight the symptoms, so they can continue to consume the very substance designed to cause pain and weakness.

It's a vicious cycle too. Since humans feed lectin-rich plants to cows, pigs, and poultry to help them gain weight, they are also getting sick with heartburn and digestive problems. What this means is that even livestock are being forced to eat an unnatural diet of corn and soybeans, without regard to their health. The lectins all end up in their milk or meat, which humans consume.

What's particularly problematic to humans are the lectins in beans and other legumes, wheat and other grains. This is because humans have yet to develop immunological tolerance to lectins. Furthermore, humans do not have the full capacity to break down these harmful proteins. As a result, numerous health problems arise, with gastric distress as the leading diagnosis.

It is not enough to know what is being eaten; it is also important to know what that plant and animal was fed with while they were being raised. This is because what they consume are passed into the body and are incorporated into human cells. The process, good or bad, has a direct effect on human health.

Are humans helpless in this war between plant and animal? The answer is a resounding no. While lectins have the ability to mess up and confuse the body's internal messaging system, humans (and animals) still have a defense system in place to help protect against the toxic effects of lectins.

The system consists of four lines of defense:

1) Mucus in the nose

2) Stomach acid

3) Bacteria in the mouth and gut

4) Layer of mucus produced by cells in the intestines.

These four lines of defense are effective in fighting off lectin. They prevent lectins from completely attacking the body. Knowing what types of foods contain lectins can help minimize their consumption and avoid devastating effects. Correcting the missteps in food consumption can help make the defense strategy work to the fullest.

The Plant Paradox Program is a microbiome- and mitochondria-centric program that recommends the right plant foods prepared the right way and eaten in the right amounts. Certain animal proteins are included in the form of wild seafood. The program is essentially a learning and application journey to remove the offending proteins in the diet to start healing the body and keep it healthy.

Key Takeaway

- Not all plants are good for the body. Some fruits and vegetables are toxic.

- Plants have defense mechanisms to prevent humans and animals from eating them. Like humans, plants have survival instincts.

- Lectin is the highly toxic protein that plants use as a weapon against predators.

- Lectins mess up the body's internal messaging system causing a breakdown in the cell processes.

- Humans have four lines of defense to protect from lectin attack. They are mucus in the nose, stomach acid, bacteria in the mouth, and the layer of mucus in the intestines.

Chapter 2

Lectins On The Loose

Unbeknownst to many plant eaters, the notorious proteins known as lectins have been creating a disturbance in human health for thousands of years. It was through trial and error that humans and animals learned what plants to avoid. But between humans and animals, it's the humans who made a discovery that would separate themselves from other creatures. It was the discovery of fire that somehow earned humans a weapon against the war with plants. With fire, plants can be prepared and cooked. The process of cooking the plants breaks down the lectins. Prior to cooking, only gut bacteria were capable of breaking down the proteins. With the use of fire, even the indigestible plant compounds called tubers were utilized.

When the last Ice Age ended, huge animals disappeared which prompted humans to look for a new source of energy. Out of the need to stock up on food, humans learned agriculture and started to cultivate grains and beans. These new resources can be stored for a long period of time, unlike fruits that needed to be consumed immediately once they ripened. The emergence of grains and legumes as staples in the human diet paved the way for the new generation of lectins to enter the human gut. Humans were ill-prepared for these newly evolved lectins that caused trouble in human health. Grains and beans were godsend because they provided the caloric requirements for humans, but they were also a curse. Needless to say, they are a double-edged sword that has changed how humans eat.

There are two types of lectins; the first one is the lectins present in one-leaf plants, and the second type are the lectins found in two-leaf plants. Grazers consume single-leaf plants, while tree dwellers consume two-leaf plants. With that said, grazers and tree dwellers have a different set of gut microbes to process two different types of lectins.

The effect of lectins is similar to that of allergy. When a person is sensitive to lectins, he or she will have a vigorous reaction. But the longer humans are exposed to the allergen, the more they are able to tolerate it. This much is true for most food and substances, but with lectins, the time frame is far longer that it took millennia for humans to build sufficient tolerance against certain lectins.

Grazers didn't always have the capacity to tolerate lectins; they had millions of years to develop a way to handle the lectins in single-leaf plants. They were able to develop a stronger immune system that can handle the effects of lectin consumption. Mice and rats have also evolved to eliminate lectins from their bodies. They also have more enzymes called proteases to break down lectins, so their gut is not always at risk from lectin attack.

Humans, on the other hand, are considered as descendants of tree dwellers who can handle lectins from consuming two-leaf plants. This ability was passed down from generation to generation. However, humans have recently been subjected to new diets and new patterns in certain foods. Although the human immune system is generally built to keep up with changes, there are four major disruptions in human eating patterns that have forced humans to accommodate a different diet. Lectins figured prominently in all of these cataclysmic changes in human diet.

The agricultural revolution shifted the human diet from mainly leaves, tubers, and animal fat to primarily grains and beans. To the human microbiome, lectins are foreign compounds. As a result, the human gut bacteria, microbes, and immune system have no experience in handling or processing the offending lectins.

Evidence of how destructive lectins are was discovered from the mummified remains of Egyptians. It was found out that they were overweight, had clogged arteries, and had dental problems. Even though people from ancient times knew that their diet rich in grains and beans were bad for their health, they still consumed them because it was a choice between survival and starvation. They found ways to minimize the toxic effects of lectin by using fermentation and other clever food preparation techniques. Civilizations owed their existence from agricultural revolution, even though it came with a price.

The second cataclysmic change is the mutation in cows. Northern European cows have undergone a mutation that caused them to produce protein casein A-1 in their milk. Before their mutation, they were producing the normal casein A-2. During digestion, casein A-1 transforms into beta-casomorphin, which has lectin-like properties. This type of protein attaches to the beta cells, which produces insulin. People who consume milk and cheese with this protein can experience an immune attack on their pancreas. It is believed that this is the likely cause of type 1 diabetes.

Although there are still A-2 cow breeds around, farmers prefer the A-1 cows because they are more robust, and they produce more milk. With farmers opting for more milk production, getting milk and dairy products from A-2 cows is getting more difficult. It is recommended to get goat or sheep milk as a safer alternative.

The third change is the emergence of plants from the New World. It is believed that lectin exposure occurred when Europeans reached the Americas. When European explorers and conquistadors brought food from the New World back to their native countries, the world was exposed to more lectins.

Europeans and Asians were introduced to a whole array of plants that contain lectins. The foods belong in the nightshade family, beans family, grains, pseudo grains, squash family, and seeds. This is rather concerning because these are the same foods that many nutritionists and health experts are recommending in the modern-day setting. Peanuts, cashews, pumpkins, acorn squash, zucchini, chia seeds, and quinoa all contain lectins.

Humans had no prior exposure to New World plants, so their gut bacteria and immune system are not able to tolerate them. As such, the body is ill-prepared to handle them, which results in numerous health issues.

The fourth change is contemporary innovations. With new knowledge and technology, new ways to process food were discovered. Genetically modified organisms (GMOs) found their way in supermarkets, including corn, rapeseed (canola), tomatoes, and soybeans. These GMOs unleash lectins at an unprecedented rate and the body is ill-prepared to handle them.

Alongside GMOs are the introduction of broad-spectrum antibiotics, chemicals, and drugs that could destroy the gut bacteria, which removes the ability of the body to process and break down these lectins. The chance to inform the immune system had been taken away, rendering the body susceptible to the ill-effects of lectin consumption.

These four factors have considerably disrupted the normal internal messaging system within the body. The onslaught of lectins made it impossible for the body to adapt in just a short amount of time. What makes matters worse, the human microbiome system is being destroyed when the body is encouraged to ingest antibiotics and artificial food products (e.g. artificial sweeteners).

Although only one of the four factors is based on modern-day discovery, the question arises why it is only now that humans are becoming more sensitive to lectins? The answer is that innovations in food processing is at a warp speed that it outpaces the body's ability to adapt in the same time frame. In the last five decades, humans are not only bombarded with lectin-rich food products, they are also inundated with chemicals—food additives, herbicides, biocides, skin-care products, and beauty products. Such overload successfully disrupts the internal messaging system that it compromises the body's ability to handle even the innocent-looking plants like grains, legumes, and other lectin-bearing plant foods.

These new information are not easy to understand and even more difficult to accept initially. This is because humans have already been conditioned to believe what they are accustomed to doing or eating. It would be difficult to step away from the generally accepted routine and switch to a relatively new eating lifestyle.

In the last 50 years, there have been significant changes in the way people consume food and use products. Unprocessed carbohydrates and leafy greens were replaced by wheat, corn, grains, and soybeans. Heavily processed food replaced home-cooked meals because of the clamor for convenience and instant service. The over-reliance on prepared foods exposes the body to questionable ingredients and artificial preservatives. Even some vegetables have become unsafe to eat due to modern farming techniques that use high-grade pesticides. These changes are compounded by the consumption of over-the-counter drugs and the use of toxic non-food products.

With such overwhelming information, it's difficult to determine the line that separates healthy foods from bad foods. Even foods that are touted as superfoods have high lectin content. So, the definition of healthy food is now a big blur. Under the Plant Paradox program, white foods are banished from the diet of the patients. This means removing flour, sugar, potatoes, and milk, and limiting brown foods to certain whole grains and legumes only. With this type of diet, patients experienced improvement in their health and well-being. But when all grains were completely removed from the diet, even greater improvements were felt by the patients. Their autoimmune diseases were cured, and their rheumatoid arthritis stopped recurring. While it may still be a long way before such diet can be embraced by the general public, the next important step is to reframe the way healthy foods is defined to include limiting the consumption of lectin-rich foods.

Key Takeaway

- Agricultural revolution, mutation in cows, introduction of plants from the New World, and contemporary innovations are the four cataclysmic changes that paved the way for lectins to infiltrate and disrupt the body and immune system

- Plant foods that are generally thought of as healthy are actually rich in lectins.

- Given the destruction caused by lectins, the concept of healthy foods should be reframed to include limiting the intake of foods with high lectin content.

Chapter 3

Your Gut Under Attack

A human's intestinal tract, mouth, and skin are home to trillions of microbes—bacteria, viruses, molds, fungi, protozoa, and worms. This may not be a pretty sight, but it paints a picture of what constitutes a human. There is clearly a lack of awareness that 90 percent of the cells and 99 percent of the genes are nonhuman. What this signifies is that humans co-exist with microbes whether within or outside the body. Human health is dependent on minute microbes and not solely on the person.

The multiplicity of microbes is called the microbiome, but scientists prefer to call it "holobiome" because it is more descriptive and inclusive. This covers the microbes in the gut, on the skin, and in the bacteria in the environment.

It is important to have a clear understanding of what's going on in the gastrointestinal (GI) tract, to better appreciate how the microbes work and function in the body system. Microbes reside in the gut and they function to break down and digest plant cell walls to extract energy and deliver it in the form of fat. Such a function is so important that without them, it would be impossible to provide the body with energy.

There are two main jobs for the microbes or guest workers. The first is to extract energy from plants that are eaten by their host. The second job is to act as a sentinel for the host's immune system. Because there is so much genetic material in the holobiome, much of the immune surveillance is delegated to these guest workers. It is akin to outsourcing the job to detect friends or foes and effectively deflecting the enemies and preventing them from infiltrating the holobiome.

Where the guest workers reside varies by species. For example, in cows and ruminants, the workers can be found in the multiple stomachs. For apes and gorillas, they reside in the intestine. For humans, they patrol along the large intestine (colon). About five pounds of these organisms live in the intestine, the skin, and in the air, which really make up the whole person. This holobiome plays a very important role in keeping the immune system, nervous system, and hormonal system in check. The organisms in the GI tract ensure that foods are digested. They are constantly at war with whatever food is ingested by the host, especially those that contain lectins.

Nonhuman cells that make up the holobiome are actually essential for a person's overall health and well-being, even if the human cells think that they are outsiders. They are quite harmless as long as they stay on their side of the *fence*. In this context, "fence" means the outside of the skin and the lining of the gut. It is crucial for the fence to be impenetrable to keep the microbes in their rightful place in the GI tract. Keeping organisms in the intestinal linings are essential for certain functions. Of course, the wall is sometimes compromised and the intestinal barrier is being breached every single day. This is because the intestinal lining not only serves to keep harmful and toxic materials out (like lectin), but it also should let nutrients in. Simultaneously accomplishing this task is tricky and it is inevitable that some unwanted organisms are able to escape and infiltrate other parts of the body.

Only the good stuff should enter the gut for the body to remain healthy. This means that only tiny single molecules of digested food should be allowed passage to the intestinal wall. Acids, enzymes, and certain microbial guest workers digest the big molecules from the food. That is, protein is broken down into amino acids, fat into fatty acids, and sugars and starches into individual sugar. These single molecules are the ones that provide energy and nutrients to the body. The mucosal cells then absorb a single molecule of amino acids, fatty acids, and sugar and release them into the veins and lymph system. So, what remains outside of the mucosal cells are the big molecules that are too big for the cells of the intestinal wall to absorb or swallow. Ideally, the big molecules shouldn't be able to get through, but in reality, they are able to because something in the system is malfunctioning. As such, the immune system alerts the body that a foreign intruder has been detected.

The gut system is efficient, but it can malfunction when there is an excess in the intake of lectins, over-the-counter painkillers, and lipopolysaccharides (LPSs). Lectins are big proteins that cannot pass through the intestinal wall, but they are so clever that they can pry apart the tight junctions between the cells of the intestinal mucosal border. When they breach the gut wall, the immune system interprets this as an attack and instructs the body to store fat and supplies in preparation for the "war". Lectins attach themselves to the border of every intestinal cell to prevent nutrients from being absorbed by the body. When this happens, the body's immune system could weaken and eventually fail.

If lectins are harmful, why are the health experts and healthcare practitioners silent about the whole thing? The simple reason is that not many doctors and nutritionists are aware of the true effects of lectins on the body.

The Plant Paradox Program have many success stories and some of them involved patients completely getting cured of their autoimmune diseases. One example is that of a twenty-year-old college student who was cured of Crohn's Disease, which is an autoimmune disease of the bowel. Many doctors are skeptical about alternative remedies and treatment because they do not know what lectins are in the first place. They wouldn't know unless they are willing to open their eyes and actually see how destructive lectins are.

The destructive ways of lectins are not immediately obvious. It would be curious to know why after eons of not being able to breach the tight mucosal barriers, lectins can suddenly penetrate the walls. The answer is in the relentless intake of nonsteroidal anti-inflammatory drugs (NSAIDs). They are painkillers that can easily be purchased from the pharmacies and supermarkets.

NSAIDs are considered godsend because they provide immediate relief from pain and other ailments. One of the most popular is aspirin. It has been proven that prolonged use of aspirin can damage the stomach lining and doctors warn patients about this. On the other hand, NSAIDs do not damage the stomach lining, so people take them to get relief from nagging pains. After careful research, it was found out that NSAIDs do not do damage in the stomach lining because they are slowly destroying the lining of the small intestine. The damaged linings allow lectins and LPSs to get into the system. The mucus that traps lectins and blocks them from passing through the intestinal border is destroyed together with the lining. When lectins flood the body, the immune system provides signals by producing inflammation and pain. And when there is pain, the immediate response is to take NSAIDs. It is a vicious cycle that can ultimately prompt people to seek stronger prescription painkillers. With the addition of antibiotics and antacids, the bad bacteria would have a field day in the system. This is the beginning of the leaky gut syndrome.

A leaky gut can lead to numerous autoimmune diseases—Crohn's disease, hypothyroidism, lupus, multiple sclerosis, ulcerative colitis, psoriasis, fibromyalgia, osteoarthritis, Sjorgren's syndrome, scleroderma, Raynaud's syndrome, and rheumatoid arthritis, to name just a few. No matter what autoimmune disease a patient suffers from, it can be cured just by addressing the main problem of a leaky gut.

The challenge is in how to start healing the leaky gut when it's in different stages of destruction. As long as the good bugs in the body outnumber the bad ones, the body is not in grave danger. But when the bad bugs dominate, there is a shift in the balance of power. The logical route is to feed the good microbes with the essential nutrients so that they can flourish. At the same time, bad microbes should be eliminated by removing foods that help them thrive.

Bad microbes feast on sugar. The more sugar is consumed, the stronger the bad microbes become. Eliminating sugar from the diet could help bring back the balance and let the good microbes prevail. While destroying the microbes, it is also important to simultaneously feed and nourish the good microbes so that they can beat the bad microbes to oblivion.

The problem is that well-meaning health gurus and nutritionists are quick to prescribe probiotics or fermented foods without properly educating the patients about the nuances of leaky gut treatment. It must then be emphasized that taking NSAIDs or acid blockers and continuing to eat lectin-rich food while trying to add good bacteria in the body would be a practice in futility. It has to be a simultaneous eradication of bad microbes and propagation of the good ones.

The modifications in the food supply, the accessibility of over-the-counter painkillers, and the changes in the environment all contribute to the disruption in the balance in the holobiome.

Key Takeaway

- The nonhuman cells (microbes) that make up the holobiome are essential for health and wellness. Disrupting the balance can trigger leaky gut symptoms.

- The gut system is efficient, but the excessive intake of lectins, over-the-counter painkillers, and lipopolysaccharides (LPSs) tips the balance in favor of the bad microbes, which causes the gut system to malfunction.

- Lectins attach to the intestinal cell to prevent the body's absorption of nutrients.

Chapter 4

Know Thy Enemy: The Seven Deadly Disruptors

The seven deadly disruptors all come together and conspire with lectins to make people fat and sick. What's even more disturbing is that lectins make the body even more vulnerable to additional negative effects of the seven disruptors, which makes the body much weaker rendering it defenseless and helpless from future attacks.

With the constant infighting of the immune army, the body becomes insulin-resistant and leptin-resistant which fall under the umbrella of metabolic syndrome. People become fat because the body is saving calories for the internal war effort. The disruptors, the lectins, and the insulin bombard and shock the body that the normal operating system falls apart and malfunctions. This is the reason why people have become fatter, weaker, sicker, and less fit compared to people half a century ago.

Disruptor 1: Broad-Spectrum Antibiotics

Healthcare and disease prevention have improved dramatically over the last sixty years. Medical technologies helped treat many diseases that were considered life-threatening just a few decades ago. But medical improvements come with their own sets of risks and dangers. They can be a double-edged sword, which is pretty much what the Plant Paradox is about. There's no better example of a medical breakthrough that has saved lives and at the same killed others than broad-spectrum antibiotics.

Developed in the late 1960s, broad-spectrum antibiotics are so potent that they can eradicate multiple strains of bacteria simultaneously. These antibiotics were touted as miracle drugs because they have saved countless lives from diseases like pneumonia and septicemia. The problem was that antibiotics kill the infection without regard to which bacterium was responsible for the infection. This form of carpet-bombing not only kills the bacteria, but it also harms the body. This is because every time a broad-spectrum antibiotic is ingested to kill infections, the good microbes in the gut are being killed too. It is concerning because it takes up to two years for the good microbes to return to the body and some may even be gone for good. Another alarming fact is that when an antibiotic is given to a child, the likelihood for the child to develop autoimmune diseases increases later in life.

Human consumption of antibiotics does not solely come from a doctor's prescription. Most of the chicken or beef sold in the United States contains antibiotics that are potent enough to kill a bacteria colony in a petri dish. The antibiotic does not care if the bacteria is good or bad, it just indiscriminately kills anything on its path. It does not have the ability to discern which ones are good bacteria and which ones are bad.

Farmers and livestock producers also give arsenic to free-range chickens to give out that "healthy" pinky blush. Everyone knows that arsenic is a poison, but not everyone is aware that it is a hormone disruptor that mimics the actions of estrogen. Corn and soybeans that are added to chicken feed also contain estrogenic substances.

Because of antibiotics, bacteria that have been relatively marginal in the past have developed into superbugs that are resistant to antibiotics. This poses a threat to vulnerable individuals whose bodies are unable to handle the bombardment of potent microbes. A widespread resistance to certain types of antibiotics could have life-threatening consequences. With the way livestock are being fed with antibiotics like Baytril, humans are likely to develop resistance to Baytril's sister drug called Cipro, which is used on humans to treat a host of bacterial infections.

By altering the human intestinal flora, antibiotics puts the body on alert mode, which increases the fat storage to accommodate all the fuel needed to fight off foreign invaders. Consuming antibiotic residues from milk products only exacerbates the effect on the body.

Disruptor 2: Nonsteroidal Anti-Inflammatory Drugs (NSAIDs)

NSAIDs have been around since the early 1970s. They were introduced to the public as an alternative to aspirin, which was adjudged as damaging to the stomach lining. The public had zero knowledge about the damaging effects of NSAIDs, but the pharmaceutical companies knew. Doctors only found out later on when camera pills were invented. They discovered that NSAIDs were damaging small intestines, which creates pathways for harmful microbes to get in. Inflammation and pain are the immediate effects. The symptoms create a vicious cycle because those who suffer from pain are prescribed the very same NSAIDs that caused the problem in the first place.

Disruptor 3: Stomach-Acid Blockers

The acid in the stomach is so potent that bad bacteria never make it out alive. Bacteria loves an oxygen-free and low-acid environment, so they stand no chance in the stomach. Without stomach acid, the disease-causing bad bacteria can outgrow and disrupt the normal gut flora. Furthermore, if there's a lack of stomach acid, the bacteria, good or bad, can creep into the small intestine where they shouldn't be. They cause trouble in the gut barrier which eventually leads to a leaky gut. When this happens, the lectins have free access to the circulatory system. The immune system shifts to "war" mode causing inflammation. This then starts the process of storing more fat to fuel the white blood cells to ward off the invaders. As a result, there is weight gain or illness.

The use of stomach acid blockers like Prilosec, Nexium, and Protonix not only stop stomach acid production, it also poisons the brain's mitochondria, which lose the ability to produce energy. This is alarming because these drugs are also proton pump inhibitors (PPIs) that breach the blood-brain barrier. This is why the over-the-counter drugs come with a warning that they shouldn't be taken for more than two weeks. Studies have shown that there is an increased risk of dementia among people aged 75 and older who had used acid blockers and PPIs. Other studies revealed that the use of PPIs is linked to chronic kidney disease.

Since the drugs reduce stomach acid, the bad bacteria that are normally killed in the stomach creates a new population of intestinal bugs that are completely foreign to the body. They replace the good normal bugs and the result is the weakening of the immune system making people under medication more prone to acquiring pneumonia. The drugs also prevent the complete digestion of protein. Since lectins are proteins, they are not being digested or processed completely, so they just swim to the gut with reckless abandon.

As a result of the incomplete digestion of proteins, the elderly—who are prescribed acid blockers—are protein deficient. This is not because they don't consume enough protein, but because they have no more stomach acid. Without this very important acid, the proteins are not transformed into amino acids that can be absorbed by the body.

Disruptor 4: Artificial Sweeteners

Regardless of how artificial sweeteners are marketed to the public, they mess up the balance in the gut holobiome. Products containing saccharin, aspartame, sucralose, and other artificial sweeteners kill off the good bacteria, allow the bad bacteria to outgrow the good ones and eventually replace the population of the good ones. When the bad bacteria take over the intestinal flora, the body system melts down. This is the start of weight gain and inflammation. There can be nothing more ironic than a food product that is supposed to help in weight loss can do just the complete opposite.

The big problem here is that the body is not able to distinguish the sweetness that came from the real sugar from the calorie-fee sweeteners. This is because the molecular pattern of artificial sweeteners fit right into the port in your taste buds that transmit sweetness. This means that it sends pleasure signal to the brain but the expected calories from the sugar don't arrive in the bloodstream and are not detected by the glucose receptors in the brain. As a result, the brain feels cheated and asks to get some more sugar that isn't sugar at all. This is how artificial sweeteners mess with the communications system in the body.

If that isn't bad enough, these fake sugars are also endocrine disruptors, which mean they interrupt the body's internal circadian clock. Cells operate on a circadian clock and so do all body functions. Even the holobiome has circadian rhythms. Sweet tastes coincide with the fruit season, which preceded the winter season where food is limited. With that said, the sweet taste is not meant to be a year-round event. So, if sugar is consumed all year round, it causes disruption in the natural rhythm, thereby causing continuous weight gain.

Although artificial sweeteners should be considered enemies. It is best to steer clear of saccharin, aspartame, acesulfame K, sucralose, neotame, agave syrup, pure cane sugar, and corn syrup.

There are friendly substitutes like Stevia, chicory root, xylitol, yacon syrup, and inulin, however, they should only be taken in moderation because they stimulate the insulin response, which makes people crave for more of the sweet taste.

Disruptor 5: Endocrine Disruptors

More commonly known as hormone disrupters, these estrogen-like substances encompass chemicals that are found in items like plastic, scented cosmetics, sunscreen, and other products that contain dichlorodiphenyldichloroethylene (DDE). Exposure to these potent agents affects humans and animals in varying ways. The effects may not even show up for years. Prolonged exposure to these agents can cause obesity, reproductive issues, thyroid problems, impairment of the development of the brain and neuroendocrine systems, diabetes, and other metabolic diseases.

More often than not, people are not aware that they are ingesting these deadly substances because they are hidden in highly processed food products. One of the culprits is preservatives. An example of this is butyl hydroxytoluene (BHT), which is commonly used in processed foods and whole-grain food products. It is necessary to add BHT because the omega-6 fat in the bran will oxidize and go rancid without the preservative. Another example is the Bisphenol A, more commonly known as BPA. This is used as an agent to make plastic heat-resistant. They are used in making plastic water bottles and teething rings used by babies. It is also used as linings for canned goods to prevent the tin from corroding. Parabens in sunscreens and cosmetics also fall under this category.

What is concerning is that many of these chemical agents make their way into products that are used everyday like deodorants, soaps, toothpaste, sanitizers and a long list of personal care products. They destroy the good microbes in the mouth, on the skin, and in the gut. They act like estrogen and change the gut flora, leading to obesity over time.

The good microbes in the mouth convert compound into a powerful chemical that dilates the blood vessels and promotes normal blood pressure. Killing off these good bugs increases the blood pressure significantly.

Another effect is the depletion of Vitamin D. The offending compounds lowers the ability of the liver to process Vitamin D, thereby preventing the regeneration of new cells in the intestinal wall. As a result, more lectins and foreign bodies are led inside.

Many of the compounds used in the foods and products are bad for the health and yet they are being consumed and used daily. Needless to say, they should be avoided, but it's really tough when there are only a few friendly substitutes. Reading the labels definitely helps form the habit of staying away from highly processed products.

Disruptor 6: Genetically Modified Foods and Herbicides

It's a known fact that herbicides, pesticides, and insecticides contain ingredients that are harmful to the body. After all, their mission is to kill annoying little species. They have contributed to the reduction of the number of victims affected by mosquito-borne diseases and have helped increase crop yield. These are the intended purposes of the use of biocides. However, their unintended effects are destructive. When humans are exposed to these poisons on a regular basis, they experience a change in the signaling process in the body. The chemicals unleash genetic programs that upset the normal messaging structure of cells in the body.

Herbicides Roundup (Monsanto) and Enlist (Dow Chemical) contain the deadly 2,4-D which is one of the ingredients in the Agent Orange, which was used by the US military in the Vietnam War as part of the country's herbicidal warfare program. Over four million Vietnamese were exposed to Agent Orange and have suffered numerous health problems as a result.

Genetically modified organisms (GMO) were created with the aim of making the plant produce more of its own insecticides, in the form of lectins, or build resistance to the notorious herbicide Roundup. This is done by injecting a foreign gene into the plants. The idea is to kill the weeds around the crop and keep the GMO plant alive. In effect, it makes GMO plants immune to Roundup or similar herbicides. It ought to be a good thing because it would help farmers get rid of weeds and pests, thereby increasing crop yield. It sounded good on paper, but the actual effect is destructive to human health.

Short-term studies done on Roundup suggested that the residual herbicides on the grains or beans do not have harmful effects on humans because humans lack the plant pathway that Roundup uses to kill weeds. With this reasoning, the FDA approved Roundup. This created two problems. First, GMO plants produce proteins and lectins that the immune systems treat as foreign invaders. As a result, the body ups the fat stores thereby causing weight gain. Second, farmers used Roundup routinely on non-GMO crops too, mainly as a desiccant. They figured that dried up dead plants make harvesting wheat, corn, beans, soybean, and canola on a fixed schedule. Desiccation helps in controlling weed, in the early ripening, and in correcting the uneven crop growth, and reducing stress in machinery and equipment. This saves farmers time and money because they can harvest in one single sweep.

The spillover effect does not stop there. Glyphosate remains on the grains, corn, and beans that are then fed to livestock. As a result, they are incorporated in their meat, fat, and milk. Humans consume the by-products together with the chemical residue and it's delivered into the gut where it deals the most damage.

Disruptor 7: Constant Exposure to Blue Light

For centuries, humans and animals acquire food in response to changes in daylight. The blue wavelength spectrum of daylight specifically affects humans. Long exposure to daylight makes humans seek more food. Conversely, long nights make people seek less food. This is why in winter months, when nights are long and days are short, stored fats in the body are being burnt. Hunting and foraging for food when the food sources are scarce is pointless because the body would just expend more calories and would find little to no food.

The body is designed to burn stored fats in the winter. The hormone called leptin, which signals that the body is full, is turned on. This season cycling between the use of glucose and fat fuel is called metabolic flexibility. The process is mediated by the blue spectrum of light. So, under the normal metabolic cycle, humans should be active during the daylight and at rest when it's nighttime.

Unfortunately, modern life no longer strictly adheres to such a cycle because the advances in technology expose humans to blue light for long periods of time. In fact, humans are exposed to blue light almost nonstop. Televisions, mobile phone, tablets, electronic device, and lightbulbs emit blue light, which interferes with sleep. What's more, it suppresses the melatonin production. Melatonin is the hormone responsible for sleep. When a person is deprived of sleep, he or she is likely to gain weight.

Blue light also emits cortisol (awake hormones) and ghrelin (hunger hormones). The genetic programming of the body associates blue light daylight, so when blue light is present all throughout the day, the body is tricked into thinking that it is perpetually in the season with longer daylight hours. The body thinks that it's summer all year long. This signals the body to prepare for the coming of winter, so the body continues to pack in the pound in anticipation for winter that will never come. The ancient rhythm has been completely disrupted that everyone lives in an endless summer. This results in frequent eating and storing of fat, eventually leading to obesity. It is recommended that exposure to light should be minimized in the evenings to help get back to the normal cycle.

Key Takeaway

- Broad-spectrum antibiotics, NSAIDs, stomach-acid blockers, artificial sweeteners, endocrine disruptors, GMOs, and blue light are the seven disruptors that are in cahoots with lectin to make people fat and sick.

- The persistent internal war happening in the gut makes the body insulin-resistant, which causes metabolic diseases

Chapter 5

How the modern diet makes you fat (and sick)

Research studies published in peer-reviewed medical journals have revealed that changing one's diet and making some lifestyle changes can result in significant improvement in overall health. Changing diet and lifestyle is the bedrock of the Plant Paradox program and the results further support the studies that have been conducted. Many of the patients under the program have cured themselves of whatever ailments that beset them. Those who have been carrying excess weight have found themselves losing the pounds without much effort.

The likely reason why people pack in the excess pounds is that they are eating the wrong foods. Under the program, the foods that are removed from the diet is more important than what is added. Little attention is given to the role of microbes or gut bugs in maintaining a normal weight. There are certain microbes that contribute to weight gain, and there are others that can cause weight loss. If the gut bugs are not doing their jobs digesting food, the body may miss out on both micronutrients and calories. One disease that is notorious for causing malnutrition is Celiac Disease.

When a person is overweight or underweight, it is a clear sign that there is a war going on inside the body. Americans have started experiencing a battle with weight gain and onset of numerous diseases. Today, 70.7 percent of Americans are considered overweight, 38 percent of which are adjudged as obese. This is quite a shocking change from two decades ago. What's worse, Americans also experience an increase in the incidence of diabetes, arthritis, cancer, heart disease, Parkinson's disease, dementia, osteoporosis, and asthma. It is estimated that one in every four people now suffer from one or more autoimmune diseases. This is despite being better fed and doing less work compared to people just two generations ago. Allergies have become so prevalent that adults and kids carry with them EpiPens because exposure to allergens, such as peanuts, has become life-threatening. In the 1960s, peanuts posed no danger to people.

The excess weight and poor health have been blamed on the Western diet, the environment, and sedentary lifestyle. While such a statement may be true, each of the reasons provided is not the primary cause of the health crisis. When diet regimens and exercise programs focus on these causes, the results, though favorable, will not be sustained. The programs may work for a few months, but they all fall apart when it reaches a certain point and that's when the regain is much more relentless.

The failure to maintain the ideal weight can be attributed to the obsessive focus on the wrong things. Weight-loss diets are so trendy that they distract people from the real issues about health. The problem with diets is that they don't fail to address the underlying problem.

The war that is happening inside the body must be ended first before the weight goes back to the normal level. The goal is not to slim down, but to heal the body. The game plan is a self-healing program that requires a change in eating habits. It necessitates learning and understanding how different foods affect the already dysfunctional internal system.

It cannot be refuted that exercise is good for overall health, but it is not effective in weight loss efforts. While it does help people maintain their healthy weight and improve cardiovascular health, it does not make people lose weight permanently.

To understand how people have become overweight and sick, it is important to know how insulin works. The main job of insulin is to open the door to any cell so that glucose could enter and provide fuel to the fat cells, muscle cells, and nerve cells. When sugar enters the bloodstream from the gut, insulin is secreted by the pancreas into the bloodstream. Once docked in the ports, the three cells tell the hormone that the message has been received and the hormone would then undock so that the port is left open for the next hormone to attach. The system is efficient and it keeps things in order. But trouble starts when lectins mimic insulin and bind to the docking ports reserved for hormones. The notorious lectins either releases the incorrect information to the cells or blocks the cells from giving the information. Either way, lectins disrupt the messaging system and all hell breaks loose. The incorrect messages (or the lack of them) result in less muscle mass, starved brain and nerve cells, and more fat than is necessary.

When the body is at war internally, it sends a signal to get more calories. This means that the more grain- and bean-based foods are consumed, the more lectins enter the body, and the hungrier the body gets. The vicious cycle leads to the body becoming insulin- and leptin-resistant. So, it's important to understand that people don't become insulin- and leptin-resistant because they are overweight; they are overweight because the body thinks it is at war and saving up calories to be used as a weapon for the internal strife. If the body thinks that it is constantly fighting with the bad microbes, then the calories will pile up because the body tries to seek and conserve more food (i.e. energy source). As such, weight gain is a result of the war instigated by lectins in the body, in the same way weight loss is a side effect of ending the war within the body.

Fat is stored in the gut because the calories need to be in the front lines to fight the lectins and LPSs. Belly fat is really in the belly because the war is right in that location. The more fat there is, the more escalated the problem is. This is dangerous because as the war continues to rage, it not only stays in the intestines, but it also spreads to the heart and brain.

There is an abundance of weight-loss diets and they do work albeit temporarily. Atkins, Dukan, South Beach, and Protein Power fall under the low-carb, high-protein diets, while Paleo and ketogenic diet are under the low-carb, high-fat, high-protein diet. Diets designed by Ornish, McDougall, Furhman, and Esselstyn are known as low-fat, high-carb diet. Followers of these diets claim that they achieved their weight-loss goals. This is a great achievement, however, some people who have managed to control their weight continued to have troubling and persisting medical issues. Some of them even have advanced autoimmune diseases and coronary problems. The only way to know the answer to this is to understand what really happens if the body is subjected to these different diet programs.

The problem with a low-carbohydrate diet (e.g. Atkins, South Beach) is that it only works in the short term. The lost pounds make a more aggressive comeback when lectin-rich carbohydrates are re-introduced to the system. Even if a person sticks to the program, the weight loss slows down significantly at a certain point. In Atkins and South Beach, people start to gain weight when they start eating grains and beans. So, they end up cutting their grains and beans consumption, which actually takes them back to step one. They are just back to where they started.

The Paleo diet is based on the faulty assumption that the early man ate large animals consistently and that's what made them healthy. It is highly unlikely that they have hunted and killed large animals for meat on a regular basis. The more realistic scenario is that they subsisted on tubers, nuts, berries, and animal protein sources such as fish, snails, insects, and small rodents. The ancestral diet was designed to accomplish simple goals—to grow and reproduce. It wasn't designed for weight loss or to prolong life span.

The Paleo diet, or any low-carb diet for that matter, can help people experience weight loss or improved health, but the favorable result was not due to the restriction of carbohydrate intake, but because of the elimination of lectin-rich foods. The real problem with the Paleo diet is that it recommends the consumption of tomatoes, zucchini, bell peppers, goji berries, peanuts, cashews, sunflower seeds, and chia seeds, which are loaded with lectins. But no one is questioning their lectin content because they are marketed as healthy superfoods.

Another popular approach to weight loss is the ketogenic diet. It was traditionally prescribed to patients who have diabetes so that they can moderate their blood sugar and insulin levels. It falls under the low-carb diet, but it relies on certain fat for the source of its calories, instead of protein. As such, people under this protein-restrictive diet experience ketosis, which is the burning of fat instead of glucose from carbohydrates for an energy boost. People who are on keto diet lose weight not because of the fat burning but in eliminating the vast majority of lectin-rich foods in their diet.

Perhaps the most popular diet among people who have heart disease or coronary artery disease is the low-fat, whole grain diet. The weight loss achieved is due to four factors:

1. Lectin-containing fats are removed (soy, peanut, canola, sunflower, etc.) as well as the polyunsaturated omega-6 which can cause inflammation

2. The elimination of fats stops LPSs to sneak through the gut wall

3. The use of whole unprocessed grains, which has lower lectin content' and

4. Consumption of organic grains that are more likely untouched by herbicides, which means the gut is able to handle gluten and prevent breach in the gut wall caused by herbicides.

Low-fat, whole-grain diets can work in the short term, but the coronary artery disease will not be reversed. In fact, it may even progress. This is because the wheat germ agglutinin (WGA) in wheat continues to attach to the endothelial lining of the coronary arteries, which the immune system attacked. So, instead of repairing the arteries, it actually causes more damage. Grains that have no WGA do not aggravate the disease. This is why the Chinese, Japanese, and Koreans have lower heart disease rates than Americans because their staple grain is rice, which has no WGA. The same is true for the Kitavans who ate taro root in large quantities; and the Africans who dine on millet, sorghum, and yams.

The American diet has changed dramatically (and for the worse) in the last century, which created medical conditions that were unheard of centuries ago. Americans, both children and adults, are significantly heavier. The high rate of obesity among children is staggering that it compelled Lisaann Schelli Gitner to explore the link between the changes in the American diet and the sharp rise in childhood obesity. Her thesis studied the US government's agricultural policies that drastically changed the food supply of an entire population. It created a new food group that includes products that are highly processed and refined. Corn, wheat, soybeans, canola, and sugar beets replaced the grass-fed meats and their fats, chickens that ate bugs, and root vegetables that were the staples before the 1960s. Real fruits were replaced with fruit juices like apple and orange juice. These foods are inexpensive, so they are accessible to everyone.

The effect was evident in the increased BMI of American children. The sharp increase correlated to the changing patterns in food consumption in the United States. Pizza and chicken are the two foods that correlated completely with the rising obesity rates in children. The pattern started in the 1970s when children started eating pizza and chicken. The more they consume, the higher the average BMI becomes. Gitner's study was not about lectins, but pizza and chicken are lectin bombs.

Pizza has at least three ingredients that are high in lectin content. They are wheat, casein A-1 cheese, and tomato sauce. Chicken, on the other hand, is fed with GMO corn and soy laced with arsenic and phthalates. The way cooked chicken adds to the problem lies in the fact that because the chicken is dipped in wheat flour breading mix and deep-fried in peanut or soybean oil. Eating chicken and pizza on a regular basis increases the lectin load, which will certainly increase body weight and may even become susceptible to different diseases. It's a health crisis that has not been addressed properly by the government. There are no changes in the policies that could reverse the effects of exposure to lectin and other harmful substances. It is up to the individual person to take back his or her body and reverse years of neglect. It is the only way to achieve a healthy life free from diseases.

Key Takeaway

- The American diet inadvertently sets people up to gain weight and develop diseases because it relies heavily on grains and beans that are rich in lectin.

- Studies show that the changing pattern of the American diet has a direct correlation to childhood obesity. The more chickens and pizzas are consumed by children, the higher the average Biometric Index (BMI).

- Many diet regimens only have short-term success because they don't eliminate lectin-rich ingredients in their meal plans such as corn, wheat, and beans.

Part 2

Introducing the Plant Paradox Program

Chapter 6

Revamp Your Habits

Since the science behind the Plant Paradox Program has already been established, it is now time to take control of one's health and body. Before one starts a life-changing experience, it is important to know the four rules that govern the Plant Paradox Program.

Rule 1: What you stop eating has more impact than what you start eating, hence what you stop eating is more important.

The foods that the body is accustomed to eating are harmful and must be completely avoided. They are the ones high in lectin content and the very reason why an individual would want to undergo the Plant Paradox Program in the first place. What goes on in the gut does not stay in the gut.

Rule 2: Pay attention to the care and feeding of gut bugs because they, in turn, will care for the feeding of the body (the person in general) because they consider the body their home.

The gut bugs' wants and needs must be satisfied so that they can do what they are designed to do, which is to maintain the balance in the holobiome. At this point, people who join the program are convinced that they needed to make changes in their lifestyle to reverse the damage caused by lectins and hormone-like substances. The gut is pretty much a wasteland because of years of consumption of antibiotics, antacids, NSAIDs, and high fat and high sugar food. Without care, the gut is overrun by bad bugs that survive and thrive in such an environment. The gut should be rehabilitated so that it can go back to being a dense "rainforest" where the good bugs can thrive.

Rule 3: Fruit might as well be candy

Fruit has been considered a health food for many years. Times have changed so much that fruits now are not the same as the fruits that the early man consumed. Eating fruit in season allowed early men to fatten up for the winter. But through agricultural advancement, fruit has become available all year round. This has changed the content of fruits that they became just as bad as eating candy.

Rule 4: You are what the thing you are eating ate

This means that eating meat, poultry, eggs, and farm-raised fish is tantamount to eating corn and soybeans because those are what industrially raised animals are fed on a daily basis. They are passed on to the body including the lectins and the residues from Roundup and other toxic herbicides.

Knowing and understanding these four simple rules will make the shift to the Plant Paradox diet less difficult and more seamless.

One might wonder if the number of calories even matter in the program. The faulty archaic rule that some diet regimens follow is that calories in *equals* calories out. This is only true assuming that all the calories are being absorbed by the body. What many people don't know is that the gut buddies have a tremendous ability to consume a lot of the calories being ingested. They are able to use the calories to create little clones that either make calories unavailable for use or change them into special fats that can boost energy. The Plant Paradox Program ensures that the gut buddies will have their fair share of calories to process. This means that participants can eat more food and still continue to lose weight. While in the program, food choices will expand as the gut heals. The body's tolerance for certain lectin-rich foods will be improved. The program has three phases and does not require calorie counting or carbohydrates counting. What's important to watch out for is the intake of animal protein.

The standard American diet includes a number of foods that contain corn. Most processed foods have corn or its by-products. Even fast food restaurants depend on corn products like corn oil, cornmeal, corn syrup, cornstarch, and other ingredients extracted from the very versatile crop. In fact, when scientists examined 480 burgers from different fast food joints and discovered that 93 percent of the meat contained the C-4 carbon, which indicates that the meat came from animals that were heavily fed with corn. With chickens, it's even worse. All chickens from fast food places come from only one source, Tyson, which feeds chickens with only corn.

Carbon test done on strands of hair from typical American revealed that 69 percent was from corn. By contrast, strands of hair from typical Europeans were carbon tested and only have 5 percent corn content. This goes to show how corn-heavy the American standard diet is. Things are getting much worse because most of the field corn being grown in the US is called Bt corn, a genetically modified version of corn wherein lectin from the snowdrop plant is inserted into the corn to make it even more resistant to insects. Once this Bt corn is ingested by food animals, they also make their way into the human body.

Osteoporosis is also linked to chickens fed on corn. Genetically modified corn cause osteopenia and osteoporosis in chickens. In fact, chickens are all crammed up in pens because their bones are too brittle from their corn diet that they ran the risk of fracturing them when they walk.

Since antibiotics are routinely given to livestock, they've become hosts to multiple forms of antibiotic-resistant bacteria. So, it is no longer surprising when there is a meat or chicken recall due to an outbreak. As more research is done, more shocking findings unfold. Perhaps one of the most concerning is the discovery that pork, beef, and cow milk are contaminated with aflatoxins. This is a by-product of molds and fungi that grow on soybeans, wheat, and corn. The compounds are so toxic that they can cause cancer and genetic changes in humans. While the US Department of Agriculture

(USDA) sets standards on how much fungal toxins are allowed in crops fed to livestock, there is no set maximum amount of these toxins that enter the finished product. Americans are consuming a high amount of aflatoxin without even knowing it.

In Rule Number 2 of the Plant Paradox Program, it is imperative to care for the friendly gut bugs. They are the gut buddies who are akin to friendly neighbors who are heavily invested in protecting the neighborhood from intruders—in this case, the bad bacteria. The objective is to protect these gut buddies and encourage their propagation. Unfortunately, with the kinds of food being consumed on a daily basis, the good bugs are pushed aside and the bad bugs are growing and thriving at an alarming rate. As a result, the good bugs go in hiding and would stay hidden for fear of being decimated by the bad bugs. To help the good bugs to come out of hiding, the bad bugs must be starved. When the right kind of food is consumed consistently and regularly, the good bugs will come out stronger and in full force. What's interesting is that if the body gets used to the proper diet of plants and the right animal protein, it will continue to crave the food that the body needs to win the war against the bad bugs. Eating habits would change for the better because the body is now controlled by a new set of microbes that will take care and protect the body from diseases.

Cravings are pure torture for people who are on high-protein, high-fat, low-carb diets. But if they make adjustments and make fish their main source of protein, the cravings will cease or will be controlled, at the very least. The fats in high-protein diets usually come from lard and saturated fats from farm animals. When LPSs in the gut attached to these saturated fats, they sneak through the wall gut and find their way into the hypothalamus, the hunger center of the brain. The inflammation in the brain triggers hunger.

Unlike Paleo and ketogenic diets, which use a lot of animal fats, the Plant Paradox Program makes use of appropriate animal fats only. As a result, the constant hunger pangs are eliminated. The program also has vegetarian and vegan options for people who are not keen to eat meat, fish, and poultry. The program convinces people that plants also offer plenty of muscle-building protein.

The Plant Paradox Program aims to achieve optimal health goals and allows the participants to manage their weight by eating foods that promote a healthy holobiome where good bugs can propagate and thrive. The program has three important phases that will help achieve these goals.

Phase 1

This phase is about cleaning and repairing the gut through the three-day cleanse. The goal is to banish the bad microbes and fortify the good ones. In three days, the gut will change significantly and be ready to move quickly to Phase 2. The transition should be immediate to prevent the bad microbes from returning.

Phase 2

The program kicks off in phase 2 and lasts for two weeks. In this time frame, the participants could expect significant changes. After six weeks, new eating habits are engrained in the system. More foods will be eliminated from the diet and new foods would be introduced.

Initially, major lectins will be eliminated from the diet. This means turning away from corn, soybeans, grains, legumes, GMO foods, and other foods that contain estrogen-like substances. Sugar and artificial sweeteners will also be removed from the diet. Industrial farm-raised poultry would be a big no-no as well. Aside from food, endocrine-disrupting products would be eliminated too.

The wrong foods would be replaced by leafy greens and certain vegetables, tubers, omega-3 fats, and foods that contain resistant starch. Protein from meat consumption is limited to just 8 ounces. Wild-caught fish that are high in omega-3 fatty acids and do not contain Neu5Gc (which damages the artery) are recommended. Only eggs from pastured or omega-3 fed chickens are allowed in the diet. Daily protein from grass-fed or pasture-raised livestock is limited to only 4 ounces because they contain Neu5Gc.

Milk and dairy products must come only from breeds of cow, sheep, and goats that produce casein A-2. As a general rule, dairy products (except ghee) must be eliminated completely.

Phase 3

In this phase, the intake of all animal protein (fish included) is limited to 2 to 4 ounces per day. It is also during this phase that intermittent fasting is introduced. Phase 3 is optional, but it is recommended to achieve maximum benefits.

For participants with diabetes, cancer, kidney failure, dementia, Parkinson's, Alzheimer's, or ALS, the Keto Plant Paradox Intensive Care Program has specific instructions on how to kick-off the healing phase.

Many vegetarians and vegans who have come to Dr. Gundry for help struggled with the diet because it was difficult for them to give up pasta, beans, and grains, even though they know those foods were making them ill. It was also a problem for Dr. Gundry because it means the program will not work on them. Fortunately, there is a workaround to this problem. **The good news is that using a pressure cooker to cook food will destroy lectins in beans and other legumes.** When pressure-cooked, beans that are stripped of their lectin content become good food for microbes in the gut. Some canned beans and legumes are pressure-cooked and the cans are not lined with BPA.

Examples of these products are Eden Foods and Westbrae Natural. When properly prepared using a pressure cooker, beans and legumes can be consumed by vegetarians, vegans, and people who could not give up eating them.

Unfortunately, the good news does not extend to wheat, oats, barley, and rye. This is because lectins in these grains are indestructible. These foods are still off-limits. It is only when lectins are destroyed that it becomes acceptable in the diet. Without lectins, the beans play a significant role in weight loss. If participants intend to go this route, they must do so in Phase 3. It is important to remember that grains are causing all the things that people are trying to get rid of, so there's really need for them to be included in the diet. Pressure cooking lectin-rich foods should only be done as a last resort measure.

Consuming protein is essential because it powers the body and builds muscle. Proteins fit for consumption are those that provide the essential amino acids that the body cannot make by itself. However, most Americans consume more protein than they need from animal proteins. Overconsumption of proteins means the body struggles to metabolize large amounts of protein into sugar. As a result, blood sugar levels skyrocket, obesity rears its ugly head, and life span is shortened. If that is not enough reason to avoid animal protein, perhaps knowing that certain amino acids from animal protein, such as methionine, leucine, and isoleucine, promote aging and speeds up cancer growth.

People tend to come up with many excuses for not committing to a health and fitness program. Excuses are barriers to a healthy and long life. Potential participants are reminded not to fall for the following excuses.

- **Excuse #1**: You are already slim, fit, and active

- **Excuse #2**: You are worried that the program requires a deep understanding of human metabolism and nutritional concepts

- **Excuse #3**: You're too old to make significant changes in your eating and other habits (or you think your loved ones are).

These excuses are unfounded myths and should not stop anyone from moving forward with the Plant Paradox program.

Key Takeaway

- The Plant Paradox Program is governed by four rules that center on the right foods to eat, where to procure them, and what to eliminate.

- The program has three phases that focus on gut cleansing, elimination of foods with lectin, introducing plant-based proteins, reduction in the consumption of animal protein, and fasting.

Chapter 7

Phase 1 Kick-Start with a Three-Day Cleanse

Phase 1 of the Plant Paradox Program starts with a three-day cleanse. The cleansing of the gut is necessary to drive out the bad bacteria. It has been established that bacteria and single-cell organisms can control appetite and trigger cravings for the wrong foods. When the invaders take over the holobiome, they need to be eliminated before they can cause too much damage in the gut.

Studies have shown that a three-day cleanse, regardless of what diet regimen is being followed, changes the kind of bacteria that inhabit the gut. However, going back to old habits can make the bad bacteria move back in within a day. So, it's important to stick with the program to achieve *sustained* success. While many diet regiments focus on the bugs in the colon, recent research studies suggest that the war between good and bad microbes are actually happening in the small intestines. The program focuses on the entire gut, so the real problem is being addressed.

What's great about the program is its flexibility. The three-day cleanse is optional. If participants prefer to start Phase 2 straight away, then it is their choice. However, it might take a little longer to achieve results without a three-day cleanse.

Phase 1 Strategies

Phase 1 not only repairs the gut so that it is conducive for new microbes to thrive, but it also repels the invaders by starving them. The complete cleanse has three components:

Component 1: On and Off the Menu

During the three-day cleanse, the following foods are NOT allowed: grains, pseudo-grains, dairy, seeds, sugar, eggs, soy, nightshade plants, roots, tubers. Inflammatory oils are also off the menu: corn oil, canola oil, soy oil. Meats are off limits as well.

The meals will consist of vegetables and small amounts of fish or pastured chicken. The recipes were developed specifically for phase 1 to cleanse the gut and prepare it for next phases. The recipes can be modified as long as the following guidelines are enforced:

Vegetables

- There is a particular emphasis on vegetables that belong in the cabbage family including broccoli, bok choy, Brussels sprouts, cabbages (any type and color), cauliflower, mustard green, and kale.

- Recommended greens are lettuce, spinach, Swiss chard, endive, and watercress.

- Other vegetables and herbs that can be added to the menu are asparagus, celery, fennel, radish, artichokes, onions, garlic, mint, parsley, basil, and cilantro.

- Ocean vegetables like kelp and seaweed are safe for consumption, including nori sheets.

- The vegetables can be taken raw or cooked. If participants are suffering from irritable bowel syndrome, diarrhea, or gut issues, it is best to cook the vegetables thoroughly to avoid any complications.

Proteins

- The only protein that should be consumed are wild-caught fish such as salmon, mollusks, or shellfish. Serving should be limited to 8 ounces per day.

- Pastured chicken is acceptable but should be limited to 4-ounce portions.

- Tempeh (without grains and hemp tofu are good alternatives as well.

Fats and Oils

- Hass avocado is recommended daily

- Use only the following oils: avocado oils, macadamia nut oil, sesame seed oil, walnut oil, extra-virgin olive oil, flaxseed oil, and hemp seed oil.

- Other good oils are MCT oil, Thrive algae oil, and perilla oil. They may be difficult to acquire in stores, so the best way to get them is through online.

Snacks

- Avocado is the recommended snack. Consume half an avocado splashed with lemon juice and a combination of the approved nuts (macadamia, walnuts, pistachios, pecans, hazelnuts, Brazil nuts, to name just a few).

Condiments and Seasonings

- The following are acceptable: fresh lemon juice, mustard, sea salt, freshly cracked pepper, herbs, and spices.

- Commercially prepared salad dressings, dips, and sauces are a no-no.

Beverages

- Make it a habit to take a green smoothie every morning. The green smoothie contains Romaine lettuce, baby spinach, mint, avocado, lemon juice, water, and stevia as a sweetener.

- Drinking 8 cups of tap or filtered water a day is recommended.

- Italian sparkling mineral water such as San Pellegrino is also recommended. Still mineral water like Acqua Panna is acceptable).

- It is recommended to drink plenty of tea (green, black, herbal) or decaffeinated coffee.

- The acceptable sweetener is stevia extract (SweeLeaf or Just Like Sugar).

Sleep and Exercise

- At least eight of hours of sleep is recommended.

- Low-impact exercise in moderation is recommended, preferably outdoors.

It cannot be overemphasized that sticking to the guidelines is key to the success of the program. Ingredients should be procured from the best source to ensure the quality of the ingredients.

- Vegetables used in the program should be 100 percent organic. Purchase vegetable only from local markets and farmers who practice sustainable agriculture

- Fresh vegetables should be in season.

- Fish and shellfish should be wild caught.

- Chicken should be pastured.

- Extra virgin olive oil should not be exposed to high heat.

- Hemp seed and flax seed oil should not be heated, so they should only be used for dressing salads and vegetables.

In the absence of organic version of vegetables, the regular veggies will suffice, but people should not expect immediate favorable results of the cleanse. The purer the ingredients, the faster the results.

Component 2: Prepare the "Soil" and Remove the "Weeds"

Starting with a clean slate is the best way to start Phase 1 of the Plant Paradox Program. This is akin to preparing the soil for planting new crops. Weeding out all the bad bacteria and toxins from the gut. The late great nutritionist Gaylord Hauser had recommended the use of an herbal laxative called Swiss Kriss. The said laxative has been used for nearly a century and has been effective in kick-starting Phase 1 of the Plant paradox Program.

Swiss Kriss's active ingredient is senna or sennosides, known for its laxative property. Other ingredients are known to destroy bad bacteria, including anise seed, calendula flower, caraway seed, hibiscus, peach leaves, strawberry leaves, and peppermint oil. Two tablets of Swiss Kriss should be taken before bedtime. It does not need to be repeated on the subsequent days. It is advisable to do this if planning to stay at home the following day. Again, this step is optional, especially to those who are concerned about the potential discomfort or side effects.

Component 3: Supplemental Assistance

Preparing the gut and killing the bad bacteria are just the first steps of the Plant Paradox Program. Introducing natural supplements into the program is not a strict requirement but it does make a difference especially to people who are suffering from digestive issues such as leaky gut, IBS, or any autoimmune condition.

Suggested supplements

- Oregon grape root extract or berberine

- Grapefruit seed extract

- Mushrooms or mushroom extracts

- Spices (cloves, cinnamon, black pepper, wormwood)

A fast cleanse in as short as three days can change the balance of microbes in the system, where the friendly bacteria would outnumber the bad ones. The change is immediate and participants will feel the difference. However, if they return to their old ways after the cleanse, the bad bacteria will find their way back in and the improvement in the gut flora will be fleeting. What's worse is that the bad bacteria will come back stronger. This is why it is important to transition immediately to Phase 2 to stop the bad bacteria from once again overrunning the healthy holobiome.

After the three-day cleanse, the body will likely miss all the inflammation-causing foods that it is accustomed to consuming. It is normal to experience hunger and low energy. It is all right to eat more than the suggested meals as long as the ingredients are in the list of acceptable vegetables. It is not advisable to eat more than two servings of avocado, fish, or chicken. If one must eat, it has to be veggies. Drink more water before turning to food when hunger persists.

The first 72 hours would most likely be a huge struggle because the body is exposed to something different. However, by Day 4, the body is ready to move to Phase 2 because there is a resurgence of energy and that the body is noticeably lighter.

Key Takeaway

- Phase 1 of the Plant Paradox Program focuses on cleansing the gut to get rid of bad microbes. It makes the gut more conducive for good microbes to survive and thrive.

- Phase 1 strategies include learning and understanding what foods to eliminate so that they can be replaced with acceptable alternatives.

Chapter 8

Phase 2: Repair and Restore

If a person is suffering from a health problem, it is not enough to slow the progress of the disease. The solution is to stop the problem in its tracks by pinpointing the cause and employing a remedy. The body has the ability to restore itself to 100 percent health and eliminating foods and other forces that prevent the body from healing itself can achieve this.

After the weeding phase of the Plant Paradox Program, it's now time to fast track the healing and shift to Phase 2, which will go on for a minimum of six weeks. The first step, which is the hardest part, is to stop eating lectin-rich foods that are drilling holes in the gut walls. The three-day cleanse has already eliminated some of the bad bacteria that had already caused massive damage. The elimination process continues and at the same time, the gut buddies are being nourished with proper foods and powerful natural supplements. The good bacteria have already come out of hiding in Phase 1 because the improved gut flora has made it possible for good bacteria to survive without threat from the bad bacteria. There will be no more disruption from bad bacteria because they have been neutralized by foods and supplements.

Withdrawal symptoms are common and may be compounded by headaches, muscle cramps, grouchiness, and depleted energy levels. However, these symptoms are just temporary. It takes about six weeks for the body to learn new habits; more so when replacing bad habits with good habits. After six weeks, things will be second nature and eating the proper foods would become automatic. Depending on how the body reacts to the first two weeks of the program, reintroducing lectin-containing food is possible as long as it is done gradually and incrementally. Ideally, these foods should not be added until the end of six weeks, but each person has a different sensitivity and tolerance so it's a case-to-case basis.

There will be a "**Just Say No**" list and a "**Yes Please**" list at the end of this book to help guide participants in the journey to a healthier and lighter body. One should keep a copy of the lists so that they refer to them when buying ingredients in the market or when struggling to figure out if a certain food is acceptable or not. Eventually, the "Yes" list would be wired in the brain that the "No" list would automatically be ignored.

The "Just Say No" is a list of foods that early man had not consumed. It was only about ten thousand years ago that these foods were considered as food to fight starvation during the times of famine. Grains, pseudo grains, and beans were not part of the daily diet of people from the ancient civilization. As such, they never had to deal with lectins from the grains and seeds.

The ancient foods have been sources of nutrients that nourished the population for millions of years. The lectins and the polyphenols in those beneficial plants, including their leaves, have been in the human diet for a long period of time that the gut microbes and the immune systems have developed a symbiotic relationship with them.

Although lectins are the reasons why there are numerous health problems in the world, not all of them are evil. It only becomes problematic because the body is not able to handle the messages that they convey. It takes a long time for modern humans to figure lectins out. It would be impossible to completely eliminate lectins from the diet, so the best thing to do is to control what can be consumed and in what amount. When it comes to health, people can't just consume lectin-rich foods and hope for the best. The Plant Paradox Program not only cleanses the body, but it also teaches how to handle lectins.

Different cultures deal with lectins in different ways. It has been established that the majority of nasty lectins are in the bran. For example, the notorious WGA found in bran makes the bread brown. Most cultures have found ways to get rid of the bran. The French have their baguettes and the Italians have their white pasta. It would be safe to say that "white is right" when it comes choosing foods from grain. Take the case of rice. It has been the staple food of about four billion people in the world. For over eight thousand years, rice has been cultivated and rice producers have made a lot of efforts to get rid of the bran. They removed the hull to create white rice because they were smart enough to know that the hull has the highest concentration of lectins. Things have changed since then and the brown whole-grain foods have been marketed as healthy foods. You can argue that food conglomerates are essentially promoting poison as a health food.

Even more poisonous are the members of the legume family, which includes beans, peas, soybeans, lentils, and other recent agricultural addition to the human diet. A bean may be small but it has the highest lectin content in any of the food groups. To illustrate how deadly these beans are, five raw kidney beans can clot the bloodstream within five short minutes. Ricin, which is the lectin found in the castor bean is so potent that a couple of molecules can kill a human being. This is why it is known to be used in espionage to poison enemies.

It doesn't take a spy to know that beans are hazardous to health. Just look at the examples from school cafeterias and restaurants. Undercooked beans can cause food poisoning outbreak. This is on top of the dangers of eating canned beans because of the BPA lining in cans. The good thing is that if they are pressure cooked, most of the lectins are destroyed leaving the nutritional content intact.

Milk is also elevated as an important health food that must be consumed on a daily basis. The truth is that milk stimulates mucus production because the body is reacting to the lectin-like casein A-1 protein.

Pseudo grains like the quinoa is one of the two worst lectin additions in the modern diet (the other one is corn). Quinoa had been used by the Incas but they had to go through a three-step detoxification process to remove the lectins in quinoa. They had to soak the quinoa first and then ferment them before cooking them. In the modern-day setting, the first two processes are not done, so modern humans are eating quinoas with poisonous lectin still intact. It's ironic that people who go on a gluten-free diet regard quinoa as the "healthier" substitute to grains. They are completely misinformed and would only suffer the consequences of their actions.

The nightshade family is also a deadly food group. This includes commonly eaten vegetables and fruits such as eggplants, potatoes, tomatoes, and peppers. The Italians did not immediately embrace tomatoes when Christopher Columbus introduced the plump tomatoes. It took two centuries before they agreed to eat them and that was only because they had learned to peel and deseed the tomatoes. They knew that the lectins are in the seeds and on the skin. When they make tomato sauce for pasta and pizza, they blanch the tomato in boiling water, remove the skin and squeeze out the seeds. They even hybridized the Roma tomato to maximize the pulp to skin and seeds ratio.

The vegetables from the squash family have a high lectin content. Cucumbers, pumpkins, and zucchini contain seeds that would have only grown during the summer months. Eating them sends signals to the brain that winter is coming, so the body is being prepared to store as many calories and fats. The lectins and the messed-up communication signals can make people fat and sick.

The oils in the "No" list are derived from seeds and beans that have high lectin content. Most of the oil products used by Americans came from GMO seeds like canola. For Phase 2, it is recommended to limit the use of saturated fats such as coconut oil and animal fats, as well as olive, avocado oil, and MCT oil. Cheese, sour cream, and heavy cream should be avoided as well during this period. Instead, the use of perilla oil is recommended because of the high content of rosemarinic acid, which helps in improving memory and cognitive functions. It also has alpha linolenic acid in high doses, which is a form of the heart-healthy omega-3 fat.

These are compelling reasons that should make people avoid lectins. So, when the "No" list says no, it really means no. There's no other way to interpret it. When the "Yes" list is finally understood, Phase 2 of the program can then move along without much resistance. For the next six weeks, the body will begin to heal as long as the offending food groups are omitted from the diet.

In Phase 2, participants should continue to plug the holes on the gut wall by doing the following:

- Eliminate foods that contain high lectin content. Vegetable with seeds, grains, pasta, bread, cereals, crackers, and other processed foods are must be omitted from the diet. The "No" list will serve as a guide on what to avoid.

- Out-of-season fruits must be avoided at all costs. If possible, don't eat fruits (except avocado) at all because they are just as bad as candy with high sugar content.

- Avoid use of saturated fast in the first two weeks. This means limiting the use of good oils (olive oil, coconut oil, avocado oil) as well, at least in the first two weeks of the program.

- Strictly follow the portion control for animal proteins. Limit to a total of 8 ounces, which can be consumed at breakfast and dinner.

- Less animal meat consumption helps reduce the intake of Neu5Gc. This applies to grass-fed and pastured livestock.

- The main protein content should be from wild fish and shellfish. Staying away from farm-raised fish like tilapia, catfish, or shrimp.

- Fish on the high food chain like sushi-grade tuna, swordfish, grouper, and tilefish should be avoided because of their high mercury content.

- Tofu and unfermented soy products must be avoided.

To feed the good microbes (gut buddies), the following must be done:

- Consume resistant starch so that the friendly gut buys can produce short-chain fatty acids and ketones which the body can absorb from the gut and be used as fuel. Resistant starches include plantains, taro root, parsnips, turnips, jicama, celery root, green papayas, green bananas, and green mangoes.

- Eat vegetables high in fructooligossacharides (FOS). FOS is a form of indigestible sugar that gut bugs thrive on. FOS can be found in okra, artichokes, onions, garlic, radicchio, Belgian endive, and sunchokes. FOS compounds are also available in powder form and as sweeteners (SweetLeaf and Just Like Sugar).

- Eat FOS-rich mushrooms to keep the gut buddies well-nourished.

- Consume dates or dried figs in limited amounts. They are high in FOS. They can be added to salads and smoothies as well.

- Eat as many leafy green vegetables as possible, and preferably those from the cabbage family (crucifers).

- Add lemon juice, vinegar, and balsamic vinegar to the meals because they contain polyphenols, which are micronutrients high in antioxidants.

- Consume ¼ cup of nuts twice daily to promote the growth of the gut buddies. Pistachios, walnuts, pecans, and macadamias are high in polyphenols and are associated with reduced risk of overall mortality.

- Take fish oil capsule before each meal because they contain omega-3 fatty acids that prevent and manage heart disease.

Changing to a healthy and mostly plant-based diet can be difficult for some people, but here are some tips on how to go about it during breakfast, lunch, snack time, and dinner.

- Breakfast doesn't have to be the time for heavy eating. A green smoothie made of fresh avocado and selected greens would suffice. Certain bars from the Yes list can be consumed, including Quest bars, Yup bars, the Human Food Bar, and the Adapt Bar. These bars contain animal protein, so the daily protein content can add up quickly. Moderation is key in any dietary plan. Under the program, the cinnamon and flaxseed muffin or coconut and almond muffin are the most popular. Planta pancake and coconut milk yogurt are two other options.

- Snacks are allowed in the morning and in the afternoon. Romaine lettuce and Belgian endive are great snack options. Limit the consumption of nut mix to just ¼ cup because nuts can be addictive and it's difficult to stop. Fortunately, there are store-bought single-serving of organic guacamole (e.g. Wholly Guacamole). They are available at Costco. Trader Joe and Whole Foods has sliced jicama to go well with the pepper-free guacamole.

- Lunch is the easiest meal to adapt to the new lifestyle. Salads are the automatic choice. Premade varieties can be purchased at most grocery stores. As for the dressing, avoid prepared salad dressing because they contain toxic oils and corn syrup. Homemade balsamic vinegar and extra virgin olive oil mix is the best option for salad dressing.

- Dinner is the time to eat animal protein. It must be kept in mind that protein from animals should only play a supporting role in daily meals and not the central one. Serving portion should be the size of the palm of the hand excluding the fingers. Wild fish and shellfish are preferred. To make the meal more filling, incorporate the animal protein into a salad.

- The gut buddies are delighted by a variety of vegetables. This is because vegetables have a unique set of phytonutrients. Frequent changes in the vegetable mix not only helps beat mealtime monotony, but it also makes the good microbes happy with the variety of nutrients.

Dietary changes are just part of the Plant Paradox Program. Over-the-counter medications and use of antibiotics must also be avoided. However, it is important to first consult with physicians and healthcare providers on the proper course to take when it comes to medications.

- Stop using stomach-acid blockers. Instead, use antacids (Tums or Rolaids) as safer alternatives. Betaine or marshmallow root and deglycyrrhizinated licorice (DGL) can also be taken to heal leaky gut.

- Eliminate NSAIDs and use Tylenol instead for pains. It is recommended to take 5-loxin or Boswellia extract, which can be found in supplements like Now D-Flame and MRM JointSynergy to treat aches and pains.

Supplements are important in the diet because they provide an additional boost of vitamins and minerals to help the body heal. The added nourishment is another layer of protection for the body against bad bacteria.

- Take 1000 mg of fish oil supplement per day. Fish oil not only protects the lining of the gut, but it also prevents dementia and neurological issues associated with aging.

- Consume vitamin D supplements to help restore gut health. To address vitamin D deficiency without going overboard, limit the intake to 5000 to 10,000 IUs. It can be increased as needed upon consultation with a healthcare professional.

- Take probiotics to restore gut flora. Targeted probiotics such as *Bacillus coagulans* (BC30), *L. reuteri* and *Saccharomyces boulardii* are recommended.

- Take betaine and grapefruit seed extract to repel invaders and help rebuild the stomach acid.

- Take indole 3-carbinol and DIM to reactivate white blood cells in the intestinal lining. Simply increasing the intake of cruciferous vegetables will also do the trick.

The results of the Plant Paradox Program can vary among participants. After six weeks, most participants can feel significant changes in their body and in their overall health, while others would probably be just starting to get used to the program. Some may be compelled to stay in Phase 2 a little longer or may not even move on to the next phase. There is always a choice depending on how participants feel about their health.

When certain changes have started to manifest, then it's time to move on to Phase 3. The changes are as follows:

- Weight loss leads to a return to normal weight

- Aches and pains have been alleviated or have completely vanished

- Brain fogs have cleared

- Persistent digestive and gut issues have disappeared and autoimmune symptoms have been abated

Key Takeaway

- Phase 2 of the Plant Paradox Program fast-tracks the healing process by nourishing the body with the right foods.

- Eliminating antibiotics, NSAIDs, and stomach acid blockers is part of the process to prevent damaging the gut walls.

- When positive changes start to manifest, the body is ready to shift to Phase 3 of the program.

Chapter 9

Phase 3: Reap the Rewards

Phase 3 can be compared to harvest time, where the fruits of labor become tangible and the sustained benefits from Phase 2 are starting to materialize. At this stage, the gut is stabilized and a noticeable weight loss can be observed. Symptoms of autoimmune diseases no longer persist and a newfound vitality shines through. Many patients of the Plant Paradox Program have attained success and have come to embrace the new lifestyle.

There are two things that participants are expected to achieve in Phase 3. The first is to ascertain that the gut is completely healed and the balance in the holobiome is achieved. The second is to test if certain lectins can be reintroduced to the system — but only if it is established that the gut bugs are all happy, healthy, and thriving in the repaired gut flora.

It is important not to rush things even if the six weeks have elapsed. If the gut is not yet ready to reintroduce lectin foods, it would show. The participants can choose to remain in Phase 2 to continue the repair and the restoration of the gut.

Through sophisticated blood tests every three months, it can be determined whether the gut flora has been restored and that the intruders and the LPSs have completely vacated the gut rainforest. But even without blood tests, participants can sense these themselves.

So, it is up to them if they want to try and reintroduce small amounts of lectin foods into their gut.

Making the decision involves determining answers to the following questions:

- Has the bowel movement returned to normal?

- Have joint pains stopped?

- Has the brain fog cleared?

- Has the skin cleared?

- Is the body's energy level increased?

- Has the quality of sleep improved? Does restlessness still occur?

- Was the weight loss (for overweight) or weight gain (for underweight) noticeable?

If the answer to all these questions is a resounding "Yes", then the body is ready to take lectin foods. However, if the answer to any of the questions is "No", it means the body is not yet ready. There's no need to be alarmed or be worried. It's better to extend Phase 2 that to prematurely transition to Phase 3.

Phase 3 does not really have a suggested duration because it is actually a lifestyle. This means staying in Phase 3 could enhance health and quality of life. The participants can increase their life expectancy without being beset by numerous health issues that usually plague old people.

These are the things that must be done in Phase 3:

- Continue to eat foods and ingredients in the "Yes" list.

- Consume more ketogenic fats (e.g. MCT oil, coconut oil) to start the fat burning process instead of being stored as fat.

- Continue to avoid the "No" foods in the list. However, this is also the best time to test lectin tolerance and reintroduce small amounts of lectins. This can be done by eating immature lectin-bearing vegetables such as zucchini, eggplant, and cucumbers. These veggies have tiny seeds, so their lectin content isn't high.

- If tolerance is observed, introduce heirloom tomatoes and pepper (peeled and seeded). Give each veggie a week to see the effects before reintroducing another vegetable.

- Introduce small amounts of pressure-cooked legumes to see the tolerance level.

- If the body and the gut are doing well even after reintroducing the lectin foods, it's time to introduce white basmati rice in extreme moderation. This is also the time to introduce pseudo-grains that have been pressure-cooked. Exclude barley, oats, rye, and wheat because they contain gluten.

- Eat less food and stop having frequent meals. This will give your gut, brain, and mitochondria the chance to rest.

- Reduce intake of animal protein to 2 ounces per day. Derive most of the protein from leaves, vegetables, mushrooms, nuts, and hemp. Keep referring to the "Yes" list and don't deviate from it.

- Continue taking the recommended supplements in Phase 2.

- Start intermittent fasting.

- Restrict calorie intake, specifically from animal protein.

- Restore daily and seasonal rhythms by going out for an hour each day to get daylight exposure.

- Get eight hours of sleep.

- Exercise regularly.

- Avoid exposure to blue light in the evenings. Use blocking strategies.

The western diet is heavy on grains and animal protein. The dangers of excessive animal protein intake have been established in two recent human studies. Both studies have concluded that meat consumption is a major contributor to obesity. It can even be worse than the effect of sugar on the body. Red meat also contains the sugar molecule called Neu5Gc which is linked to cancer and heart disease.

The fact is that eating animal protein is not necessary to achieve good health. Those who have avoided animal protein have the greatest longevity among people who have lived long lives. The risk of developing Alzheimer's correlates directly to the amount of meat consumption. This should be enough warning to deter people from over-consuming animal protein.

Another important addition to the new lifestyle is fasting. Contrary to popular belief, fasting is not dangerous. Certain cultures practice fasting on a regular basis not because it is trendy or people want to cleanse their gut, but because food is not always readily available. During fasting, ketones are burned for energy instead of glucose. This is evidence that the body can adapt to using ketone as a main source of fuel when sugar from protein and carbohydrates are not available. Most of the big religious denominations practice some form of fasting. Mormons who fast once every week are found to live longer than their non-fasting counterparts.

It is hard to quit animal protein because it has been part of the modern human diet for so long. It's not something that people can turn away from with just a flick of the switch. Fortunately, there is a way to restrict animal protein consumption without feeling deprived. Limiting calories and avoiding animal protein for just five days each month gives the optimal result. This is done by following the vegan version the Phase 1 cleanse but extending it to five days instead of three. The vegan version only has 900 calories. After the five-day low calorie, no animal protein diet, proceed to do the Phase 3 guidelines for the rest of the month.

Another alternative is intermittent fasting (IF). This type of fasting is focused on a twice a week fasting that cuts calories from 500 to 600 per day and eating normally for the rest of the week. The meals can be anything from the "Yes" list as long as the calorie intake is reduced significantly. To get an idea of how much (or how little) the food looks like, it is equivalent to three approved protein bars per day, or between 6 to 8 pastured or omega-3 eggs, or five bags of Romaine lettuce with three tablespoons of homemade olive oil and vinegar dressing. The choice depends on the person. As long as it is within the program guidelines, it's all good.

According to Dr. Dale Bredsen, a leading dementia researcher at UCLA, the longer a person goes between meals, the more the body develops metabolic flexibility in the mitochondria. It is recommended to fast for 16 hours. So, if a person finishes dinner at 6:00 p.m., the next meal (brunch) would be at 10:00 a.m. the next day. The farther the fast is extended, the better the results.

Key Takeaway

- Phase 3 continues the repair and restore phase but focuses on fat burning, intermittent fasting, and eliminating animal protein from the diet.

- Phase 3 also allows the reintroduction of lectin foods to see how the body is able to tolerate them.

Chapter 10

The Keto Plant Paradox Intensive Care Program

Some of the participants of the Plant Paradox Program are suffering from various physical issues. Some of them have diabetes, cancer, and kidney failure, while others are afflicted with Parkinson's, dementia, or other neurological diseases. They are patients that need intensive care because the energy-producing organelles of their cells are in total shock. The regular dietary requirements may not be enough, so they have to undergo the Keto Plant Paradox Intensive Care Program.

Patients who are in the advanced stages of various diseases have got their systems shut because of the breakdown of the intestinal barrier caused by lectins and the LPSs. The body is completely surrounded by intruders. This is particularly true for patients diagnosed with dementia and Parkinson's. The specialized white blood cells known as glial cells protect the nerve cells so well that when they detect the presence of lectins, they circle around the neurons. Unfortunately, the tight guarding of the glial cells does not allow even the simplest form of nourishment, so the nerve cells and the nerve die from lack of sustenance. While that is happening, the notorious lectins and LPSs alters how the mitochondria process sugars and fats.

The mitochondria have a symbiotic relationship with their host cells so that they can produce ATP, the energy-generating molecule that is needed for the cells to function. The mitochondria have their own DNA, just like their host cells. They divide at the same time and share the workload. The mitochondria shoulder the workload that pertains to handling the calories being consumed. They use sugars and fats to produce ATS in the assembly line called the Krebs cycle. Just like any worker in an assembly line, the mitochondria can only do so much work and need downtime to recharge.

The circadian clock worked well for the mitochondria. They worked non-stop during the day, turning sugars and protein into ATP. When nighttime comes, mitochondria slow down and cut back on the workload. They don't immediately grind to a halt, they go on a slow burn because they depend on the ketones instead of the sugar and protein, which are absent during night time (assuming the body is asleep and not eating).

Unfortunately, with the change in lifestyle, working hours, and eating habits, the mitochondria and the team are constantly overworked. They are forced to process an insane amount of calories, 24 hours a day, 7 times a week. Working for 365 days non-stop can take a toll even on the mitochondria. As a result, they refuse to carry the extra workload. So more unprocessed sugar and protein are dumped in the body as fats. The stress causes the mitochondria to lose energy. The brain, on the other hand, keeps sending a message to the mitochondria to find more sugar and turn them into energy because the brain is starving from the energy deficit. When this scenario persists, cancer cells start to move in and use all the sugars that are just lying around. This is what overconsumption does to the body. It causes a metabolic mix up that messes up the clockwork process of the body system resulting in massive fat storage.

It would seem that the easy way out is cut back on sugar and protein so that the strain on the mitochondria is lifted. It's easier said than done. The Atkins diet makes the body get into ketosis, which is the burning of the stored body fat. Unfortunately, the mitochondria cannot process fat directly from the fat cell. A required component is the hormone-sensitive lipase. It is an enzyme that has the ability to turn the stored fat into a usable form of fat called ketone. High insulin blocks the hormone-sensitive lipase so it does not have access to the stored fat. Cutting back on sugar does not eliminate insulin because all the proteins are still there, unprocessed. This is the scenario that can be expected when a person goes on low-carb, high-protein diets such as Atkins, South Beach, and Paleo.

To fix this ketone conundrum, both sources of insulin-rising calories must be significantly reduced, which means dropping consumption of sugar and protein at the same time. This would cause insulin levels to drop and would also significantly reduce the workload of the overworked mitochondria.

Since the body is unable to make ketones, the workaround is to eat and drink ketones that plants have already made available for consumption. Ironically, eating fat (from plants) is the key to unlocking the fat storage.

Medium-chain triglycerides (MCT) that are found in MCT oil are 100 percent made of ketones. Another fat from plants is solid coconut oil, which contains 65 percent MCT. Other sources of ketones include red palm oil (50 percent ketone), butyrate (from butter), and ghee or clarified butter.

The reason why people on a ketogenic diet are not getting into or maintaining the state of ketosis is that while they are consuming the good MCT fats, they are also eating a lot of animal protein. As long as ketogenic dieters are eating bacon, sausages, and high-fat cheeses, the stored fat will not be broken down into ketones.

In the case of cancer, the mitochondria in the cancer cells are not capable of using ketones to generate ATP. They are also unable to combine sugar and oxygen to generate ATP. Instead, cancer cell mitochondria depend on the highly inefficient system of sugar fermentation similar to the process used by yeasts and bacteria. With that said, they need eighteen times more sugar to grow and divide. Cancel cells also favor fermenting sugar into fructose than glucose. This is another reason why fruits, which are high fructose content, should not be part of any diet. To kill cancer, the cancer cells must be starved out of existence.

The Keto Plant Paradox Intensive Care Program has its own set of acceptable foods. They are similar to the standard care program, which needs just a little bit of tweaking to address issues relating to diseases.

Here are some specifics on what to do when under the intensive care program:

- Macadamia nuts are the preferred nut; other nuts can take a backseat.

- Sugar-free coconut milk frozen dessert is still in the list, but cross out goat's milk ice cream.

- Dark chocolate now has to be at least 90 percent cacao (vs. the 72 percent from the regular program). Lindt has dark chocolates with 90 percent cocoa.

- Limit animal protein intake to just 4 ounces per day. This is just the same size as a deck of cards. Wild fish, shellfish and mollusks are the preferred source of animal protein.

- Cancer patients should eliminate animal proteins altogether. Animal proteins have a higher concentration of amino acids that cancers use to grow and divide.

- Egg yolks are pure fat that is needed for brain function. A three-yolk egg omelet cooked in ghee or coconut oil with sliced avocado, onions, and mushrooms is a great way to start the day. Adding turmeric and macadamia add more flavor and extra nutrients.

- Vegans can have Haas avocado, hemp seeds, and walnuts— they are good sources of fat and proteins.

- Greens and resistant starches are fat-transport devices. It is a way to deliver fat into the body. Drenching salads with olive oil, perilla oil, or macadamia nut oil is recommended. Also, mixing MCT oil with other oil is a great way to get the much-needed ketones. Use a one-to-one ratio. MCT oils are flavorless so they can also be added on smoothies and shakes without the funky taste.

- To boost fat burning, patients have to take a tablespoon of MCT oil every few hours. Since cancer or diabetic patients do not have the metabolic flexibility to access and use the stored fat, they need something to burn the fat. MCT oil or coconut oil are the best options. Without these oils, patients may experience weakness, dizziness, or brain fog.

- Single-serving packets of coconut oil are now available in stores so that it is easy to get a shot of healthy oil while on the go. Look for any of the following brands: Artisana, Carrington Farms, Kelapo, and Spectrum.

The Keto Plant Paradox Intensive Care Program is a diet for life for people who have cancer, diabetes, kidney disease, neurodegenerative diseases, or any autoimmune disease. If all health markers have improved in two to three months, it is all right to switch the regular program and skip Phase 1. Depending on how the body is doing, patients can always switch back and forth. Falling off the wagon could happen, but the important thing is that one can always climb back up and keep fighting the good fight. Once health significantly improves, there's no reason not to stick to the program for life.

Key Takeaway

- The Keto Plant Paradox Intensive Care Program is specifically designed for people diagnosed with cancer, diabetes, autoimmune diseases, and neurodegenerative diseases.

- The program focuses on healing the body by starving cancer cells and making sure that the brain and body receive sufficient nourishment.

- The program has no time period because it promotes a lifestyle change and a diet plan for life.

Chapter 11

Plant Paradox Supplement Recommendations

Nutrient supplementation is a crucial component of the Plant Paradox Program. This is because the foods—vegetables, fruits, grains—no longer provide the necessary nutrients to meet the daily requirements for a healthy life. Scientists have known about this fact since 1936 because they have studied the soil where these agricultural foods have been harvested. Since then, the situation had become worse. The soil had been depleted of vitamins and minerals because of the aggressive use of petrochemical fertilizers, herbicides, pesticides, and Roundup.

It is not possible to get the required nutrients without taking supplements. The foods do not always provide the right amount of nutrients so using supplements can give the needed boost to keep the body well-nourished.

Vitamin and mineral deficiency are common among Americans and those that follow the western diet. Here are some supplements that must be added to the diet.

- **Vitamin D_3.** Americans are deficient in vitamin D_3. The normal vitamin D blood level is between 70 to 105 ng/ml for serum 25-hydroxyvitamin. It is recommended to take 5000 IUs of vitamin D_3 daily. For people with autoimmune disease, the dosage should be increased to 10,000 IUs daily.

- **The B Vitamins.** The B vitamins are mostly produced by gut bacteria if the gut flora is thriving. But if the gut is damaged, chances are there is a deficiency in methylfolate (active form of folic acid) and methylcobalamin (active form of B_{12}). B vitamins lower the level of homocysteine in the bloodstream, which causes damage to the inner lining of the blood vessels. It also has links to elevated cholesterol levels. It is recommended to take a daily dose of 1000 mcg tablet of methylfolate and 1000 to 5000 mcg of methyl B_{12}.

- **Polyphenols.** When metabolized by the gut bacteria, polyphenols prevent atherosclerosis by blocking the formation of trimethylamine N-oxide (TMAO) from animal protein carnitine and choline. It also actively dilates the blood vessels. Polyphenols are found in grape seed extract, resveratrol, and pine tree bark extract. The suggested doses are between 25 to 100 mg, depending on the chosen supplement. Other polyphenol supplements include green tea extract, cocoa powder, cinnamon, and pomegranate.

- **Green Plant Phytochemicals.** Gut buddies love greens and there are not enough greens to satisfy them so supplements are needed. Greens have phytochemicals that help reduce hunger. It is recommended to take 500 mg spinach extract capsule per day. Taking two capsules of modified citrus pectin per day helps reduce elevated galectin 3 levels, which is a marker for myocardial and kidney stress. Avoid phytochemicals in powder form because most of them contain wheat, barley grass, or oat grass, which are not acceptable.

- **Prebiotics.** These are food for the probiotics so that they can survive and grow. Prebiotics feed the good microbes and staved the bad ones. It is recommended to take the prebiotic inulin powder daily.

- **Lectin Blockers**. It is possible to accidentally consume food with lectins while under the Plant Paradox Program. There are compounds that absorb lectins so that they don't reach the gut wall. It is recommended to take glucosamine and MSM in tablet form. Other lectin-blocking supplements include Osteo-Bi-Flex, Move Free, and D-mannose. Dr. Grundy has formulated Lectin Shield, which contains nine ingredients to absorb or block lectins. The suggested dosage is two capsules before a suspect meal.

- **Sugar Defense.** Sugar is everywhere and it's quite impossible to avoid them completely. There are compounds that change how the body and insulin handle and process the sugars that are consumed. These compounds include chromium, zinc, selenium, cinnamon bark extract, turmeric extract, berberine, and black pepper extract. They are all in Dr. Gundry's Glucose Defense supplement.

- **Long-Chain Omega-3s.** Many people are deficient in the omega-3 fatty acids EPA (eicosapentaenoic) and DHA (docosahexaenoic acid). This is very worrying because it has an effect on the brain, which is about 60 percent fat. Half of the fat in the brain is DHA and the other half is AA (arachidonic acid). A great source for AA is egg yolks. Those with high levels of omega-3 fats in their blood have a better memory. Fish oils help repair the gut and prevent LPSs from crossing the gut border. It is important to buy molecularly distilled fish oil which comes from anchovies and sardines. It is recommended to achieve 1000 mg of DHA per day. Some good brands include Kirkland Signature Fish Oil. It has no fishy aftertaste. Other recommended fish oil supplements are OmegaVia DHA 600 and Carlson's Elite Gems.

- **Other supplements.** There are many supplements that can be taken depending on what the person is deficient in. Supplements can help address deficiencies and promote health. The list is long, but supplements for brain health, circulation support, liver support, hair loss, estrogen blocking, prostate support, mood support, and longevity are available in health stores and online. For patients under the Keto Plant Paradox Intensive Care Program, magnesium and potassium are added to the dietary plan. These two elements keep muscles from cramping.

There is the notion that taking supplements will reverse illnesses and heal the body completely. This is a misconception that must be corrected. Supplements provide great benefits and they enhance the Plant Paradox Program. However, they should not be treated as substitutes for the program.

Key Takeaway

- Nutritional deficiency can be addressed by taking supplements. It would be impossible to get all the required nutrients from the foods, so supplements are necessary to fill the gap.

- Supplements enhance the Plant Paradox Program and give measurable benefits.

Part 3

Meal Plans and Recipes

Chapter 12

Meal Plans and Recipes

Phase 1 Sample Meal Plan: Cleanse

Breakfast: Green Smoothie

Snack: Romaine Lettuce Boats Filled with Guacamole

Lunch: Romaine Salad with Avocado and Cilantro-Pesto Chicken

Snack: Romaine Lettuce Boats Filled with Guacamole

Dinner: Lemony Brussels Sprouts, Kale, and Onions with Cabbage Steak.

Phase 2 Sample Meal Plan: Repair and Restore

Breakfast: Green Smoothie

Snack: ¼ cup raw nuts

Lunch: Pastured chicken breast and cabbage slaw wrapped in lettuce leaves with sliced avocado

Snack: Romaine Lettuce Boats Filled with Guacamole

Dinner: Spinach Pizza with a Cauliflower Crust; mixed green salad with avocado vinaigrette dressing

Phase 3 Sample Meal Plan: Modified Vegan Fast: Reap the Rewards

Breakfast: Green Smoothie

Snack: Romaine Lettuce Boats Filled with Guacamole

Lunch: Vegan version of Arugula Salad with Chicken and Lemon Vinaigrette, using hemp tofu

Snack: Romaine Lettuce Boats Filled with Guacamole

Dinner: Vegan Version of Cabbage-Kale Sauté with Salmon and Avocado, using grain-free tempeh

Sample Meal Plan for the Keto Plant Paradox Intensive Care Program

Breakfast: Green Smoothie with 1 tablespoon MCT oil

Snack: ¼ cup macadamia nuts or Romaine Lettuce Boats Filled with Guacamole

Lunch: Quorn Chik'n Cutlets and cabbage slaw wrapped in lettuce with 2 tablespoons avocado mayonnaise and sliced avocado. Drink 1 tablespoon MCT oil.

Snack: 1 packet single-serving coconut oil or 1 tablespoon MCT oil

Dinner: Spinach Pizza with a Cauliflower Crust smothered with olive oil and MCT oil

Vegan alternative: Marinated Grilled Cauliflower Steaks; mixed green salad topped with avocado and keto vinaigrette.

The Plant Paradox Program Recipes

Selected recipes from the Plant Paradox Program are presented here. The recipes are easy to prepare and takes a few minutes to do. The ingredients can be replaced with vegan or vegetarian alternatives.

Green Smoothie

Serves 1

Total time: 5 minutes

Ingredients:

1 cup romaine lettuce, chopped	4 tablespoons freshly squeezed lemon juice
1/2 cup baby spinach	3 to 6 drops of stevia extract
1 mint spring with stem	¼ cup ice cubes
½ avocado	1 cup tap or filtered water

Place all ingredients in a high-powered blender. Set to high and blend until smooth and fluffy. Add more ice cubes until desired consistency is achieved.

Arugula Salad with Chicken and Lemon Vinaigrette

Serves 1

Total time: 15 minutes

CHICKEN

1 tablespoon avocado oil

4 ounces boneless, skinless pasture-raised chicken breast, cut into ½ -inch-thick

strips

1 tablespoon freshly squeezed lemon juice

¼ teaspoon sea salt, preferably iodized

Zest of ½ lemon (optional)

DRESSING

2 tablespoons extra-virgin olive oil

1 tablespoon freshly squeezed lemon juice

Pinch sea salt, preferably iodized

SALAD

1½ cups arugula

MAKE THE CHICKEN

1. In a small skillet, heat the avocado oil over high heat.

2. Place the chicken strips in the hot skillet. Sprinkle with the lemon juice and salt.

3. Sauté the chicken strips for about 2 minutes; turn them and sauté for another 2 minutes until cooked through. Remove from the pan and reserve.

MAKE THE DRESSING

Combine the olive oil, lemon juice, and salt in a mason jar with a tight-fitting lid. Shake until well combined.

TO SERVE

Toss the arugula in the dressing and top with the chicken. Add the lemon zest (optional).

VEGAN VERSION

Replace the chicken with grain-free tempeh, hemp tofu, or a cauliflower "steak." For the cauliflower steak, sear the ¾-inch-thick cauliflower slice in avocado oil over high heat until golden brown on both sides.

VEGETARIAN VERSION

Substitute chicken with acceptable Quorn products.

Romaine Lettuce Boats Filled with Guacamole

Serves 1

Total time: 5 minutes

Ingredients

½ avocado

1 tablespoon finely chopped red onion

1 teaspoon finely chopped cilantro

1 tablespoon freshly squeezed lemon juice

Pinch sea salt, preferably iodized

4 romaine lettuce leaves, washed and patted dry

Instructions

1. Using a fork, mash the avocado, onion, cilantro, lemon juice, and salt in a bowl until smooth.

2. Scoop an equal amount of the guacamole into each lettuce leaf.

Romaine Salad with Avocado and Cilantro-Pesto Chicken

The cilantro pesto can be made in advance. It can be stored in the fridge for three days. Basil and Parsley are great substitutes for cilantro. For the dressing, double the ingredients if making two batches.

Serves 1

Total time: 15 minutes

CHICKEN

1 tablespoon avocado oil

4 ounces boneless, skinless pasture-raised chicken breast, cut into ½ -inch-thick

strips

1 tablespoon freshly squeezed lemon juice

¼ teaspoon sea salt, preferably iodized

PESTO

2 cups chopped cilantro

¼ cup extra-virgin olive oil

2 tablespoons freshly squeezed lemon juice

¼ teaspoon sea salt, preferably iodized

DRESSING

½ avocado, diced

2 tablespoons freshly squeezed lemon juice

2 tablespoons extra-virgin olive oil

Pinch sea salt, preferably iodized

SALAD

1½ cups chopped romaine lettuce

MAKE THE CHICKEN

1. In a small skillet, heat the avocado oil over high heat.

2. Place the chicken strips in the hot pan and sprinkle with the lemon juice and salt.

3. Sauté the chicken strips until cooked through on both sides (about 2 minutes).

4. Remove from the pan and reserve.

MAKE THE PESTO

Place the ingredients in a high-powered blender. Process on high until very smooth.

MAKE THE DRESSING

1. Toss the avocado in 1 tablespoon of the lemon juice and set aside.

2. Mix the remaining 1 tablespoon lemon juice, the olive oil, and salt in a mason jar with a tight-fitting lid.

3. Shake until well combined.

TO SERVE

Toss the romaine in the dressing. Arrange the avocado and chicken over the lettuce and spread the pesto on top.

VEGAN VERSION

Replace the chicken with grain-free tempeh, hemp tofu, or a cauliflower "steak," a ¾-inch-thick cauliflower slice seared over high heat in avocado oil until golden brown on both sides.

VEGETARIAN VERSION

Substitute chicken with acceptable Quorn products.

Lemony Brussels Sprouts, Kale, and Onions with Cabbage Steak

Any type of kale can be used. Remove the stems before chopping. If using baby kale, there's no need to remove the stems.

Serves 1

Total time: 20 minutes

Ingredients

4 tablespoons avocado oil

One 1-inch-thick red cabbage slice

¼ teaspoon plus 1 pinch sea salt, preferably iodized

½ red onion, thinly sliced

1 cup Brussels sprouts, thinly sliced

1½ cups chopped kale

1 tablespoon freshly squeezed lemon juice

Extra-virgin olive oil (optional)

Instructions

1. Heat a skillet over high heat. Add 1 tablespoon of the avocado oil.

2. Reduce heat to medium and sear the cabbage slice until it is golden brown on one side (approximately 3 minutes). Flip and brown it on the other side.

3. Season with salt

4. Remove and place the cabbage on a plate.

5. Wipe the skillet clean with a paper towel and return to the stove top.

6. Heat 2 tablespoons of the avocado oil in the skillet over medium heat.

7. Add the onion and Brussels sprouts. Sauté until tender

8. Add the remaining 1 tablespoon avocado oil, the kale, and lemon juice, and sauté until the kale is wilted.

9. Season with the ¼ teaspoon salt.

10. To serve, top the cabbage "steak" with the sautéed vegetables. Drizzle with olive oil, if desired.

Spinach Pizza with a Cauliflower Crust

Serves 2

Prep time: 30 minutes

Cook time: 35 minutes

CRUST

Extra-virgin olive oil for greasing the pan

1 small head cauliflower, cut into small florets

1 pastured or omega-3 egg, lightly beaten

½ cup shredded buffalo or goat mozzarella

½ teaspoon sea salt, preferably iodized

½ teaspoon cracked black pepper

½ teaspoon dried oregano

TOPPING

¾ cup shredded buffalo or goat mozzarella

½ cup cooked and drained spinach

Chopped vegetables of your choice (optional)

¼ cup grated Pecorino-Romano cheese

Pinch sea salt, preferably iodized

Instructions

1. Rice the cauliflower by chopping the cauliflower evenly. Don't pulverize it. You can grate the cauliflower using a cheese grater. This will yield about 3 cups.

2. Transfer to a microwave-safe dish and microwave on high for 8 minutes, until cooked. Allow to cool, stirring occasionally.

3. Place a rack in the middle of the oven. Heat the oven to 450°F.

4. Grease a 10-inch ovenproof frying pan with olive oil.

5. Place the cooled riced cauliflower in a dishtowel. Gently twist and squeeze to remove excess water and moisture.

6. In a mixing bowl, combine the rice cauliflower, egg, mozzarella, salt, pepper, and oregano. Mix well.

7. Press the mixture evenly in the frying pan.

8. Crisp the cauliflower crust over medium heat for a few minutes. Transfer to the oven and bake until golden (about 15 minutes).

9. Let it cool for 5 minutes and add the topping.

10. Scatter the mozzarella evenly over the pizza base and spread the spinach over this. Add any additional vegetables (from the "Yes" list).

11. Sprinkle with the Pecorino-Romano cheese and add a pinch of salt.

12. Bake for an additional 10 minutes, until the cheese has melted.

VEGAN VERSION

Replace the egg with 1 VeganEgg. Replace the cheeses with Kite Hill Ricotta "cheese".

Cabbage-Kale Sauté with Salmon and Avocado

Other wild-caught fish or shellfish can be used as the protein base. If using chicken, make sure it is pastured. Bok choy or Napa cabbage can be used instead of green cabbage.

Serves 1

Total time: 20 minutes

Ingredients

½ avocado, diced	1½ cups finely sliced green cabbage
3 tablespoons freshly squeezed lemon juice	½ red onion, thinly sliced
4 pinches sea salt, preferably iodized	3 ounces wild-caught Alaska salmon
3 tablespoons avocado oil	

Instructions

1. Toss the diced avocado in 1 tablespoon of the lemon juice and season with a pinch of salt. Set aside.

2. Heat a skillet over medium heat. When it is hot, add 2 tablespoons of the avocado oil and the cabbage and onion. Sauté until tender, about 10 minutes, stirring occasionally.

3. Season with 2 more pinches of salt. Using a slotted spatula, remove from the skillet and set aside.

4. Add the remaining 1 tablespoon avocado oil to the skillet, raise the heat to high, and add the remaining 2 tablespoons lemon juice and the salmon.

5. Sear the salmon until cooked through.

6. Season with salt.

7. To serve, top the sautéed cabbage and onions with the salmon and avocado.

VEGAN VERSION: Replace the salmon with grain-free tempeh, hemp tofu, or a cauliflower steak.

VEGETARIAN VERSION: Substitute salmon with acceptable Quorn products.

Marinated Grilled Cauliflower Steaks; mixed green salad topped with avocado and keto vinaigrette.

Avocado oil, perilla oil, or macadamia nut oil can be used instead of olive oil.

Serves 4

Prep time: 15 minutes

Cook time: 10–15 minutes

Ingredients

½ cup extra-virgin olive oil, plus additional for serving	¼ teaspoon cayenne pepper
2 teaspoon minced onion	Sea salt, preferably iodized
½ teaspoon garlic powder	Cracked black pepper
2 teaspoons Italian seasoning	Juice of 1 lemon
2 heads cauliflower	

Instructions

1. Place the ½ cup olive oil, the onion, garlic powder, Italian seasoning, and cayenne pepper in a medium bowl. Add salt and black pepper to taste and the lemon juice.

2. Whisk to combine. Transfer to a shallow pan.

3. Using a large chef's knife, cut off the cauliflower stems flush with the head.

4. Place the stem ends down on a cutting board. Slice each cauliflower in half. Then cut into slices ½ to 1 inch thick (steaks).

5. Turn on the exhaust fan if cooking indoors. Heat the grill to medium, or place a grill pan over medium-high heat on the stove top.

6. Using tongs, dip the cauliflower steaks in the marinade.

7. Place on the grill or grill pan and cook 5 to 8 minutes on each side, until browned on the outside and tender inside. Transfer to a serving platter. Adjust the seasonings and serve with more olive oil.

Key Takeaway

- The recipes can be altered to cater to vegans and vegetarians.

- For patients under the Keto Intensive Care Program, MCT oil and other healthy oils are added.

The Yes Please List

List of acceptable foods

Oils:

Algae oil	Macadamia oil	Perilla oil	Sesame oil
Olive oil	MCT oil	Walnut oil	Flavored cod liver oil
Coconut oil	Avocado oil	Red palm oil	

Sweeteners:

Stevia	Monk fruit	Xylitol
Inulin	Luo Han Guo	
Yacon	Erythritol	

Nuts and Seeds

½cup/day Macadamia	Pistachios	Coconut	Flaxseeds
Walnut	Pine nuts	Coconut Cream Hazelnuts	Hemp seeds
Pecans	Pecans	Chestnuts	Sesame seeds
Hemp protein powder	Psyllium	Pine nuts	Brazil nuts

Others:

Olives	All
Dark Chocolate	72% or greater
Vinegars	All without added sugar
Herbs and Seas	All (except chilli pepper flakes), Miso
Fat Bomb Keto	Adapt bar, coconut and chocolate

Flours

Coconut	Chestnut	Tiger nut
Almond	Cassava	Grape seed
Hazelnut	Green Banana	
Sesame	Sweet potato	

Ice Cream

- Coconut
- Milk/Dairy Free frozen dessert with 1 gram of sugar

Foodles

Capello's fettuccine	Shirataki noodles	Miracle rice
Pasta Slim	Miracle noodles and kanten pasta	

Dairy Products

A2 Milk	Goat butter	Goat and Sheep kefir	High-fat Switzerland cheese
1.oz cheese or 4.oz yogurt per day	Goat cheese	Sheep cheese (plain)	Buffalo mozzarella (made from buffalo milk)
French/Italian butter	Butter (grass-fed French or Italian)	Coconut yogurt	Organic heavy cream
Ghee	Goat Brie	High-fat French/Italian cheeses such as triple-cream Brie	Organic sour cream
Organic cream cheese (high-fat dairy doesn't have casein)			

Wine & Spirits

- Champagne (one 6 oz glass per day)

- Red (one 6 oz glass per day)

- Aged spirits (1 oz.)

Fish

Any wild caught

2 - 4 oz per day

White fish	Alaskan halibut	Crab	Lobster
Freshwater bass	Hawaiian fish	Scallops	Calamari/squid

Alaskan salmon	Shrimp	Oysters	Mussels
Canned tuna	Sardines	Anchovies	

Fruit

- Avocado or all berries in season, and sparingly

Vegetables

Cruciferous	Broccoli	Brussels sprouts	Cauliflower
Bok choy	Napa cabbage	Chinese cabbage	Swiss chard
Arugula	Watercress	Collards	Kale
Green and Red cabbage	Radicchio	Raw sauerkraut Kimchi	Nopales cactus
Celery	Onions	Leeks	Chives
Scallions	Chicory	Carrots	Carrot greens
Artichokes	Beets	Jerusalem artichokes	Hearts of palm Cilantro
Okra	Asparagus	Garlic	Leafy greens
Romaine	Red and green leaf lettuce	Kohlrabi	Mesclum
Spinach	Endive	Dandelion greens	Butter lettuce
Fennel	Escarole	Mustard greens	Mizuna
Parsley	Basil	Mint	Purslane
Perilla	Algae	Seaweed	Sea vegetables
Mushrooms			

Resistant Starches

(In moderation)

Siete brand tortillas	Bread and bagels made by Bakery Paleo Wraps made with coconut flour	Paleo coconut flakes cereal	Green plantains
Green bananas	Baobab fruit	Cassava	Sweet potatoes or yams
Rutabaga	Parsnips	Yucca	Celery root
Glucomannan	Persimmon	Jicama	Taro roots
Turnips	Tiger nuts	Green mango	Millet Sorghum
Green papaya			

Pastured-Raised Poultry

2-4oz per day

(avoid farm-raised)

Chicken	Turkey	Ostrich	Pastured or omega 3 eggs (4 yolks daily or 1 egg white)
Duck	Goose	Quail	Dove Grouse

Plant-Based Meats

Quorn	Hemp tofu	Hilary's root
Veggie burger	Tempeh (grain-free only)	Chinese cabbage

Meat

(Grass fed and grass finished 4oz per day)

Bison	Wild game	Venison Boar	Elf
Pork	Lamb	Beef	Prosciutto

The Just Say "No" List Of Lectin-Containing Foods

Refined Starchy Foods

Pasta	Rice	Potatoes	Potato chips
Milk	Bread	Tortillas	Pastry
Flours made from grains and pseudo	Cookies	Cereal	Sugar
Agave	Splenda	SweetOne or Sunett NutraSweet	Sweet n Low
Diet drinks	Maltodextrin		

Vegetables

Tomatoes (unless peeled, deseeded)	Cucumbers (unless peeled, deseeded)	Peas	Sugar snap peas
Legumes	Green beans	Chickpeas	Soy
Tofu	Edamame	Soy protein	Textured vegetable
All beans including sprouts	All lentils		

Nuts and Seeds

Pumpkin	Sunflower	Chia
Peanuts	Cashews	

Fruits/Veggies

All fruits (except in season fruit)	Ripe Bananas	Zucchini	Pumpkins
Squashes	Melons	Eggplants	Tomatoes (unless peeled, deseeded)
Bell peppers (unless peeled, deseeded)	Chili peppers (unless peeled, deseeded)	Goji berries	

Non-Southern European Cow's Milk Products

Contain casein a-1 Yogurt	Greek yogurt	Frozen yogurts	American Cheese
Ricotta	Cottage cheese	Kefir	Casein protein powders

Grain or Soybeans-fed Fish- Shellfish- Poultry Beef-lamb and Pork, Sprouted Grains, Pseudo Grains and Grasses

Whole grains	Wheat Einkorn	Wheat Kamut	Oats
Quinoa	Rye	Bulgur	Brown rice
White rice	Barley	Buckwheat	Kashi

Spelt	Corn	Corn products	Cornstarch
Corn syrup	Popcorn	Wheatgrass	Barley grass

Oils

Soy	Grapeseed	Corn
Peanut	Cottonseed	Safflower
Sunfower	Partially hydrogenated vegetable or canola	

37916492R00075

Made in the USA
San Bernardino, CA
05 June 2019